D1434384

IMPROVING HEALTH THROUGH HUMAN RESOURCE MANAGEMENT

The process of engagement and alignment

Ruth Boaden

Mick Marchington

Paula Hyde

Claire Harris

Paul Sparrow

Sarah Pass

Marilyn Carroll

Penny Cortvriend

LIVERPOOL JOHN MOORES UNIVERSITY
Aldham Robarts L.R.C.
TEL. 0151 231 3701/3634

LIVERPOOL JMU LIBRARY

3 1111 01318 6588

The Chartered Institute of Personnel and Development is the leading publisher of books and reports for personnel and training professionals, students, and all those concerned with the effective management and development of people at work.
For full details of all our titles, please contact the Publishing Department:
Tel: 020 8612 6204
E-mail: publish@cipd.co.uk

To view and purchase all CIPD titles:
www.cipd.co.uk/bookstore

For details of CIPD research projects:
www.cipd.co.uk/research

IMPROVING HEALTH THROUGH HUMAN RESOURCE MANAGEMENT

The process of engagement and alignment

Ruth Boaden
Mick Marchington
Paula Hyde
Claire Harris

MANCHESTER BUSINESS SCHOOL, UNIVERSITY OF MANCHESTER

Paul Sparrow

LANCASTER UNIVERSITY MANAGEMENT SCHOOL, LANCASTER UNIVERSITY

Sarah Pass
Marilyn Carroll
Penny Cortvriend

MANCHESTER BUSINESS SCHOOL, UNIVERSITY OF MANCHESTER

© Chartered Institute of Personnel and Development 2007

All rights reserved. No part of this publication may be reproduced, stored in an information storage and retrieval system, or transmitted in any form or by any means, electronic, mechanical, photocopying, recording or otherwise without written permission of the Chartered Institute of Personnel and Development, 151 The Broadway, London SW19 1JQ

First published 2008

Cover and text design by Sutchinda Rangsi-Thompson
Typeset by Paperweight
Printed in Great Britain by Short Run Press, Exeter

British Library Cataloguing in Publication Data
A catalogue record for this book is available from the British Library

ISBN-13   978 1 84398 201 2

Chartered Institute of Personnel and Development,
151 The Broadway, London SW19 1JQ

Tel: 020 8612 6200
Website: www.cipd.co.uk

Incorporated by Royal Charter. Registered charity no. 1079797.

CONTENTS

ACKNOWLEDGEMENTS

The research team are indebted to the many people who have contributed to this research:

❖ the members of the Advisory Group, who have been constructive and encouraging throughout

❖ Professor Bonnie Sibbald, University of Manchester, for methodological advice and substantial contribution throughout the study

❖ the case study organisations – and their partners and contractors – without whom this research would not have happened

❖ the many NHS staff who have participated in workshops at various times during the research and freely contributed ideas and comments

❖ the NHS HR professionals who took time to read and comment on a draft of this report and gave us the benefit of their experience as HR practitioners.

Within Manchester Business School we have appreciated the administrative support of Lyndsey Jackson and Jackie Kan. Additional data-gathering and analysis from Stephen Mustchin and Anastasia Kynighou has been very helpful.

LIST OF ABBREVIATIONS

AfC   Agenda for Change

ANOVA   analysis of variance

CBI   Confederation of British Industry

CIPD   Chartered Institute of Personnel and Development

DH   Department of Health

ESR   electronic staff record

FTE   Full-time equivalent

HPWP   high-performance work practices

HRM   human resource management

MH   mental health

NPM   New Public Management

PCT   Primary Care Trust

PFI   Private Finance Initiative

LIST OF FIGURES AND TABLES

FOREWORD

How can people management and development help NHS organisations achieve their goals? This report details the findings from a major research project on improving health through human resource management sponsored by the Chartered Institute of Personnel and Development (CIPD), the Healthcare People Management Association (HPMA) and the Department of Health.

The report is the result of a detailed study in a number of NHS settings. Manchester Business School carried out its field-based research during 2006 in six case study organisations from the NHS acute, mental health and primary care sectors. Over 170 interviews were conducted with NHS staff, ranging from support staff to clinical staff through to directors.

Recognising that responsibility for delivering NHS services is not the preserve of directly employed staff, a number of interviews with staff from partner or contractor organisations also took place. Qualitative methods and associated data analysis were used to develop insights into how human resource management (HRM) influences performance.

The research findings emphasise the importance of the psychological contract in mediating this relationship and disclose that having their expectations met has an important positive impact on staff performance. The data suggests that organisations should recognise that individuals' emotional responses are part of the process leading to individual performance, and that enabling and encouraging a supportive workplace has to be a management priority.

The report also offers valuable insights into how the idea of 'performance' is interpreted by individuals working in the Health Service. It finds that individuals see their own performance as being concerned with how they do their work, which then leads to outcomes for patients. Many struggled to find a link between their own individual performance and that of the organisation – perceived to be assessed using 'targets'. Helping bridge this perception gap could be a powerful tool for organisations.

Organisations as a whole should be looking at how they can use people management to drive high performance. Consequently, the findings and recommendations of this report clearly have relevance beyond the HR community. The findings from this latest research confirm the vital role of front-line managers in effectively bringing to life people management processes and practices. There are also important messages for board members, senior management, and performance and workforce managers.

In Chapter 1 the authors suggest how you might 'dip in and out' of the report in accordance with your specific interests and perspectives. We hope the evidence-based material in the report will provide an impetus to re-examine and tackle the issues and challenges you face in your own organisation, and we wish you luck on your journey.

Chartered Institute of Personnel and Development
Healthcare People Management Association
Department of Health

EXECUTIVE SUMMARY

The issue of how human resource management (HRM) contributes to the performance of organisations is one that is increasingly important. This research addresses the question 'How can HRM help NHS organisations to achieve their goals?' It shows that HRM influences performance through a process involving individuals that is more effective if each stage of the process is aligned with the next, and if HRM engages with individuals throughout the process. The research was conducted in six case study organisations from the NHS acute, mental health and primary care sectors during 2006, with over 170 interviews carried out as well as a small number of interviews with staff from partner or contractor organisations. Qualitative methods and associated data analysis methods were used to develop insight into *how* HRM influences performance.

The results of the research show that:

❖ Organisational strategy varied greatly, as did HRM strategy and structure and the arrangements for cross-organisational contracting; there was no evidence for any one 'best' way of organising HRM.

❖ HRM content was similar in each organisation although the priority given to different practices varied depending on organisational strategy. Managers were vital to implementing HRM and recognised its importance but often had little involvement with the development of HR policies, and struggled to balance their work.

❖ Individual perceptions of HR showed practices were grouped into those that support *professional development* through appraisal, training and career development, *employee contribution* through communication, teamworking and employee involvement, and *the*

employee 'deal' through recruitment, pay, non-monetary rewards, work–life balance and job security.

❖ The expectations of individuals at work can be both explicit (ie openly discussed) and tacit (ie taken for granted or not openly discussed), and are concerned with HR practices, help and encouragement, infrastructure, and enabling patient care. Having expectations met led to effective patient care.

❖ Most individuals thought their employers expected them to get the job done. Examples of going beyond employer expectations were described, often motivated by a desire to provide care for patients.

❖ Individual performance was concerned with *how* an individual does her/his work, which then leads to outcomes for patients. Organisational performance was perceived as being assessed using 'targets' that were seen by some to be in conflict with patient care – many individuals being unable to describe a link between their own individual performance and that of the organisation. However, some did describe performance for individuals, the organisation and the NHS as a whole, in terms of patient care and the effective use of resources

If HRM is to influence performance, then the organisation has to

align:

❖ all elements of strategy with the overall vision and direction of the organisation, and with the role of individuals; this must be explicit, led from the top, and be consistent

❖ the working environment and individual expectations of support because this influences individual performance

❖ feedback mechanisms and content with roles, so that performance frameworks focus on *how* healthcare is provided

❖ HR function resources, staffing and other elements of infrastructure with the demand for healthcare in order to support managers and staff in performing effectively.

communicate:

❖ the vision for the organisation effectively, with honesty and staff involvement in times of organisational change

❖ that the organisation has a culture in which it is acceptable to discuss volume and content of work. Although individuals may at times work beyond employer expectations in terms of hours, this should not be something expected routinely by employers.

understand:

❖ the competing priorities and the managerial capability of line managers

❖ the effect that organisational reputation has on individual motivation

❖ that emotional response is a part of the process leading to individual performance

❖ the expectations that individuals have of their employers

❖ that individuals are supported by colleagues and working effectively in teams to do what their employer expects

❖ *why* and *when* individuals go beyond expectations in terms of both what they do and how much time they spend. If this highlights underlying system issues, these should be resolved

❖ the implications for both the individual and the organisation of having some staff who do not believe anything is beyond employer expectations.

When working with partner and contractor organisations, the organisation must *align* positive attitudes towards providing patient care with the goals and values of the NHS, supported by good working relationships. Alignment of principles and ways of working with partner organisations must be supported by details of policy, practice and *communication* mechanisms, and may involve joint monitoring by both parties.

If HRM is to influence performance, then the HR function must

translate and adapt:

❖ national guidance on HRM as well as HR policies, along with the rationale for their use and guidance on implementation, so they are clear and understandable. HR practices will require different emphases depending on the organisational strategy and the needs of individuals

❖ the requirements of the organisation into specific roles that place realistic demands on individuals.

align:

❖ its structure with the operating units which comprise the organisation, as well as ensure consistent understanding of HRM as 'people management' throughout the organisation.

❖ HR practices and processes to key organisational goals, so that staff are encouraged to contribute to these

❖ individual and organisational performance through competency frameworks which link these levels clearly.

communicate:

❖ with a wide range and level of staff in the development of HR policies

❖ meaningful feedback about performance through mechanisms that are effective and timely.

understand specific issues which influence performance, and then take action. These issues include:

❖ the key role of line managers in people management, which requires appropriate knowledge, skills and appraisal to be effective

❖ the way in which individuals perceive the relationship between HR practices

❖ the way in which teamwork and line managers can be effective in supporting individuals who have problems with workload

❖ the fact that staff higher up the organisation have a better understanding of how their role fits with the goals of the organisation.

Key enablers of this process include relationships with colleagues/managers/support/leadership as well as infrastructure – resources and staff. Professional ideology enables performance that might otherwise not be achieved. Access to a range of HR practices is also important at each stage. This research shows that there is no one 'best way' for HRM to operate in NHS organisations. Instead, HRM must become increasingly sophisticated in engaging with a range of stakeholders to enable improvements in performance.

SETTING THE SCENE

❖ **This report describes the results of research into the way in which HRM can influence performance in organisations – addressing the question 'How can HRM help NHS organisations to achieve their goals?'**

❖ **The NHS has a vision of promoting health, reducing health inequalities and delivering the best possible care with the resources available.**

❖ **Characteristics of the NHS which influenced the research included: its status as a public sector organisation, and the ways in which it is different from other public sector organisations; its structure, which includes both commissioning and provision of healthcare; its status as a service provider; the high level of professional autonomy of its staff; and the societal context within which it operates.**

WHAT DOES THIS CHAPTER COVER?

This chapter sets the scene for the rest of the report and contains:

❖ the key elements of the research (more detail on the framework used is given in Chapter 2)

❖ the context of the research: the NHS in England

❖ a summary of the six case study organisations within which the research was carried out – a brief overview here is followed by more detail in Chapter 3

❖ a brief outline of the methods used to gather data: these are described in more detail in Appendix 1

❖ the key characteristics of the individuals interviewed, including the range of professions and levels and type of organisation from which they were drawn, and some basic demographic data.

INTRODUCTION

The current vision for the NHS in England (Department of Health, 2007; p.2) is:

to promote health, reduce health inequalities and deliver the best possible care for the population with the resources available.

'Focus and consistency of purpose' (DH, 2007; p.2–3) is continuing to enable the devolution of the way in which change is delivered to a local level so that ultimately

local organisations and patients create an inbuilt dynamic for continual service improvement.

This will in turn mean that the current top-down approach to performance management will ultimately have less importance, although the transition is going to take some years. The need to better understand the relationship between the NHS as a whole, the organisations which it comprises and those it works in partnership with, the individuals who provide NHS care and performance at each of these levels is a current issue, and one that will remain in future, whatever the mechanisms used to assess and manage performance.

THE OBJECTIVES OF THE RESEARCH

The main research question is:

How can HRM help NHS organisations achieve their goals?

Our approach is summarised in a simple diagram (Figure 1, on page 2), which formed the basis for the framework we used to gather and analyse data from the case study sites. It is further elaborated in Chapter 2 of this report.

❖ We interpreted 'goals' to be summarised as 'improving patient care' in the context of the NHS, although we did recognise that this does not always tie in explicitly with the performance framework/objectives by which NHS organisations are assessed. The underlying assumption is, however, that by achieving these objectives, patient care will be improved: the focus of the NHS vision (see *Introduction* above).

Figure 1 ✤ HRM and performance

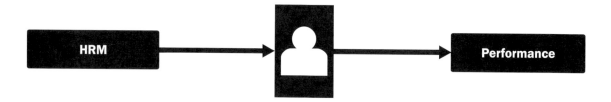

We focused on 'how' HRM influences performance rather than 'why', and took an approach based on process theory, which offers explanations of why a sequence of events unfolds over time in a particular way (Van de Ven and Poole, 2002) and is usually qualitative. We considered the process by which various elements of HRM (including HR practices) were interpreted and put into practice.

We did, however, also stipulate that one of the outputs from the research should be the identification of constraints and enabling factors for effective HRM, including context.

Following from the review of literature in the first phase of this research, we concluded (Hyde *et al*, 2006a; p.84) that:

It is possible that the key factor determining the effect of HRM on performance is the impact on the individual; the wide range of studies carried out so far have often not explored this in detail.

We therefore determined that this would be the focus of our empirical research.

WHAT THIS REPORT IS ABOUT

This report analyses empirical data from six case study organisations, which was gathered in the second phase of a research project which covered in total the period November 2004 to July 2007.

The report on the first phase – an extensive review of the literature and consultations with subject matter experts – was published by the Chartered Institute of Personnel and Development (CIPD) in January 2006 as a full research report (Hyde *et al*, 2006a), and as a briefer Change Agenda (Hyde *et al*, 2006b).

Following the first phase of the study, six NHS Trusts which had a history of high performance or recent improvement to high performance were selected for detailed case study research.

Data from the case study organisations was collected

during 2006. Interviews were conducted with individuals in the case study sites including interviews with staff from partner and contractor organisations. A range of organisational levels and professions were covered in these interviews. A number of meetings were also observed.

Three workshops with NHS HR practitioners were held in early 2007 to explore the implications of the findings from the empirical research.

During the period of the research, the team was also involved in the publication of a resource summarising the evidence for the ten HR high-impact changes (Department of Health, 2006a).

Dissemination activities also took place throughout the research project which enabled discussion and exploration of the findings with a variety of academic and practitioner audiences.

The research was sponsored by the Department of Health, the Chartered Institute of Personnel and Development and the Healthcare People Management Association.

THE KEY ELEMENTS OF THE RESEARCH

HRM: we have used the concept of the HRM system (Bowen and Ostroff, 2004). This comprises both the *HRM strategy* for the organisation and the *HRM content* – specific HR polices and practices. Use of this concept aims to build shared, collective perceptions, attitudes and behaviours among individuals (see Chapters 4, 5 and 6).

The individual: we have used the concept of the psychological contract between employers and employees (Rousseau, 2001) to explore individual perceptions of the relationship between HRM and performance (see Chapters 7 and 8). Understanding what expectations individuals hold and what they believe the other party expects in return is important in exploring the role that HRM can play in improving performance, especially in terms of direct patient care. Meeting individual expectations is a necessary but not sufficient precondition for effective individual performance which may then lead to organisational performance.

❖ Performance: we consider that performance can be described both as enacted behaviour – ie what an individual does – and something measured in some way – ie an assessment of what is done – while recognising that 'each of these meanings tends to invoke the other' (Scott *et al*, 2003; p.107) such that there are inextricable links between them. We use both subjective and objective means of describing performance in terms of individuals and organisations.

The relationship between these elements has been described using a framework developed as a result of the analysis of the data we gathered during this research, using a process of induction (see Chapter 2). This is a process framework which recognises the influence of external factors on the relationship between HRM and performance at all stages, as well as the links between organisational and HRM strategy (Bowen and Ostroff, 2004).

THE CONTEXT OF THE RESEARCH

This HRM–performance relationship operates within a context that is at a macro level concerned with the public sector in England, and the NHS in particular. The key contextual issues that influence this research, which has been carried out within the NHS in England, are:

❖ the NHS is a public sector organisation

❖ the NHS is a service provider

❖ the healthcare sector is 'different'

❖ the NHS is a 'professional' organisation

❖ the NHS operates in a changing environment

❖ the NHS has a direction of travel.

The NHS is a public sector organisation

As a public sector organisation the NHS is subject to constraints, political influence, authority limits, scrutiny and ubiquitous ownership (Backoff and Nutt, 1992). However, the development of the New Public Management (NPM) concept (Hood, 1991) has highlighted the ways in which the public sector may have been influenced by private sector practices. NPM is characterised (Glynn and Murphy, 1996; p.125) by:

the adoption of private sector management concepts and styles, the introduction of quasi-markets and contracting processes and the application of explicit standards and measures of performance.

Others (Boyne, 2002a; p.97) go further in describing particular approaches relevant to this research:

Figure 2 ❖ The NHS in England

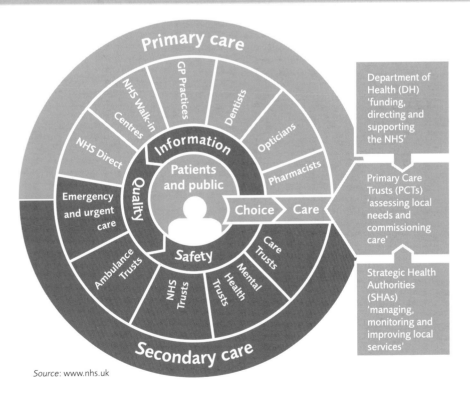

Source: www.nhs.uk

In particular, public managers should seek to emulate the supposedly successful techniques of their private sector counterparts (eg management by objectives, total quality management, devolved management and performance-related pay).

FOUNDATION TRUSTS

Foundation Trusts are autonomous organisations, free from central government control. They decide how to improve their services and can retain any surpluses they generate or borrow money to support these investments. They establish strong connections with their local communities – local people can become members and governors. These freedoms mean NHS Foundation Trusts can better shape their healthcare services around local needs and priorities. NHS Foundation Trusts remain providers of healthcare according to core NHS principles: free care, based on need and not ability to pay

Source: www.monitor-nhsft.gov.uk

THE ORGANISATION OF THE NHS

The NHS in England is organised as shown in Figure 2 on page 3.

Not all the organisations that provide NHS care are comprised solely of staff employed by the NHS. In terms of primary care, PCTs directly employ a relatively small number of staff in managerial positions but are increasingly moving towards a focus on commissioning rather than providing care. Primary healthcare services are otherwise delivered by a wide range of independent provider organisations – general practices, community pharmacies, dentists and opticians – that provide services to the NHS under contract and employ their own staff. Primary care is perhaps the most diverse part of the NHS in terms of employment arrangements.

NHS Trusts (often known as 'acute hospitals') employ most of the NHS workforce. Although there is an increasing amount of contracting-out of services provided by NHS Trusts and Mental Health Trusts, or of support services, where not all staff are therefore employed by the NHS (see Chapter 4), this is not the majority of staff. Many NHS Trusts (and some Mental Health Trusts) are now becoming Foundation Trusts. There were 65 Foundation Trusts in England (mid-2007) which remain within the performance inspection system.

The NHS is a service provider

The NHS provides healthcare in various ways and to various sectors of the population. Although many of the principles of organisation and management apply to manufacturing and service organisations, there are others specific to services, and some that are more challenging in a service environment.

THE CHALLENGES FACING MANAGERS IN SERVICE ORGANISATIONS

❖ Managing multiple customers – including a wide range of 'stakeholders'

❖ Managing the experience and the outcome

❖ Managing in real time – a service cannot be 'stored' to be used later

❖ Co-ordinating different parts of the organisation

❖ Knowing, implementing and influencing strategy.

Derived from Johnston and Clark (2005)

The healthcare sector is 'different'

Within the public sector, an argument can be made that the healthcare sector is different – an argument that does not simply apply to healthcare in the UK, where healthcare organisations are described (Ramanujam and Rousseau, 2006; p.811) as showing

striking fragmentation and turbulence that impede their capacity to provide quality care …

WHY IS IT DIFFICULT TO RESOLVE ORGANISATIONAL PROBLEMS IN HEALTHCARE?

❖ The mission of the organisations are multiple and potentially conflicting – being developed from the demands of clinical need, community services, staff, research and financial viability. Assessing these multiple missions then requires multiple dimensions, which generates additional challenges.

❖ The workforce is comprised of 'multiple professions socialised elsewhere' (Ramanujam and Rousseau, 2006; p.814) – professional groups influenced by their professional training and identity, which results in strong professional identification and weak organisational identification (Meyer *et al*, 1993). See also the section below.

❖ The external environment is complex, with multiple stakeholders. These include healthcare commissioners (who are not the patients who receive the service), the patients themselves and their families, as well as government and professional associations (eg the British Medical Association, representing doctors).

❖ The environment within which healthcare is provided is complex, ambiguous, dynamic and local – with increasing professional specialisation, demands for standardisation of clinical work as well as flexibility, the continuous emergence of new 'evidence' to support or discredit existing ways of working, and variation in performance between individual units within a single organisation.

Derived from Ramanujam and Rousseau (2006)

FEATURES OF THE PROFESSIONAL ORGANISATION

❖ Professionals have considerable autonomy and discretion, because their work involves the application of knowledge and expertise to complex problems.

❖ Professionals are loyal to their profession and committed to their clients rather than to their employing organisation.

❖ Professionals work independently, without reference to each other or to management.

❖ Managers cannot develop strategy independently but must persuade professionals to support and champion initiatives.

❖ High-quality work is based on internalised values, beliefs and aspirations, developed through training, rather than on formal bureaucratic controls.

Buchanan *et al* (2007; p.253)

The NHS operates in a changing environment

Like many public sector organisations, there are significant changes within the NHS which affect the workforce (Hyde *et al*, 2006). Some of the broader contextual changes include (DH, 2007):

❖ Rising expectations – patients would like the 'control, choice and convenience they expect in other parts of their lives' (DH, 2007; p.5) from the NHS

❖ Demographics – an ageing population has implications for how services are organised, and these influences also have implications for the provision of staff

❖ Changes in medical technology – these create new costs and change the way services are configured, as well as affecting the skill mix and job design of the people involved in the process

❖ Variations in quality, safety, access and value for money – across different areas of the country. These variations are essentially between elements of organisational performance – a focus of this research.

The NHS is a 'professional' organisation

Like organisations in accountancy and law, healthcare organisations are 'professional' (Mintzberg, 1979, 2003) and characterised by high levels of professional autonomy. Details of the implications of this are well summarised elsewhere (Buchanan *et al*, 2007) but some of the elements relevant to this research are shown in the following box below.

The NHS has a direction of travel

Although the NHS could be described as an 'organisation', we have previously argued (Hyde *et al*, 2006a; p.48) that:

The NHS does not have a single document which is termed a strategy – although informal evidence suggests that many staff would regard the NHS Plan as the 'strategy' in that it has driven most of the changes in the NHS since its launch in 2000.

The NHS Plan (DH, 2000) was intended to make services more responsive to patients with its first phase focusing on 'building workforce and physical capacity and tackling issues of major concern to the public' (DH, 2007; p.4). The second phase starts in 2007/8, moving towards a

self-improving system in which change is led and driven by clinicians and other staff, and managers at a local level, responding to the needs of their patients and the public.

THE KEY ELEMENTS OF THE CURRENT NHS STRATEGY

❖ More choice and voice for patients, giving patients real power, backed up by strong commissioning

❖ More diverse providers, with more freedom to innovate and improve services and more competition on quality

❖ Financial incentives to improve care and promote sound financial management and best value

❖ National standards and regulation to guarantee quality, safety and equity

❖ Sustained focus on information management and technology to underpin the reforms and deliver better, safer care.

DH (2007; p.5)

CAN WE LEARN FROM FAILURE?

This research provides an adjunct to prior research on performance failure and turnaround in health services, which identifies HRM as a central feature in organisational failure. Specifically, failing organisations have poor staff management, low morale, poor clinical–managerial relationships, lack of involvement of staff in problem-solving, staff turnover and recruitment problems (Harvey *et al*, 2004; Fulop *et al*, 2004).

CAN WE LEARN FROM SUCCESS?

What does HRM look like in successful organisations? Research by West *et al* (2006) has found that HR practices are associated with lower patient mortality rates in acute hospitals in the UK. Purcell *et al* (2003) conducted case study research (one site being an Acute Trust in the NHS) into the HRM–performance link and reported that line managers are important because they 'bring policies to life'. The current research therefore involves healthcare organisations that were relatively successful in conventional terms and identifies features of HRM in these organisations.

THE CASE STUDY ORGANISATIONS

The six case study organisations comprised two Acute Trusts, two Mental Health Trusts and two Primary Care Trusts representing a diverse spectrum of Health Service provision, locations and organisational types (see Table 1, opposite). This research took place as PCTs were being restructured across England reducing the total number from 303 to 152. Consequently, it was more difficult to gain agreement from PCTs to participate in the research, although ultimately, one PCT unaffected by the restructuring and one that was affected by the restructuring but still willing to participate were used as case studies – both were medium (2-star) performers.

Further details of the performance history, organisational and HRM strategy and systems for each case-study organisation can be found in Chapter 3.

HOW WE GATHERED THE DATA

Details of the research methods are contained in Appendix 1 of this report. The research approach was predominantly qualitative, in line with the research question which asks how HRM influences performance.

❖ Qualitative methods are typically utilised in case study research because of the nature of the 'how' questions under consideration and the need for in-depth exploration of concepts (Yin, 1994).

❖ Case studies involve detailed investigation of phenomena in context, to highlight the context and processes which

Table 1   ❖   The case study organisations

	Organisation type	Population served	Annual turnover (£million)	Number of staff	Key characteristics
			Information from 2005/6 Annual Report unless otherwise specified		
1	Acute Trust	300,000	£190	4,500	Few recent structural changes compared to other NHS organisations, most service provision in-house
2	Acute Trust	400,000	£144	2,700 + 1,000 in the PFI partner	A recent major redevelopment programme including a PFI hospital and resultant outsourcing of ancillary services
3	Mental Health Trust	600,000	£85	1,860 FTE	Foundation status awarded May 2006
4	Mental Health Trust	700,000	£100	1,830 FTE	Foundation status awarded May 2006
5	Primary Care Trust	380,000	£465	3,500	Internal reconfiguration including separation of provider and commissioner elements as a result of merger in 2006
6	Primary Care Trust	150,000	£241	1,200 (internal HR information, 2006)	Close partnership with the local council, including social care, with joint provision of some services

illustrate the issues being studied (Hartley, 2004). The aim is to understand how behaviour or processes are influenced by and influence context (p.323). Case studies are good for understanding everyday practices and their meaning to those involved (p.325); they can focus on one or more organisation or groups or individuals.

❖ It has also been argued that case studies are an excellent means of obtaining insights into the application of managerial interventions (Yin, 1994; Maylor and Blackmon, 2005).

❖ Within a case study design researchers may start out with a rudimentary theory or framework and develop this framework as research progresses to make sense of the data, as we did in this research. Yin (1994) argues that discovery should occur during the research process rather than following a rigid research design, and at the same time bias and selectivity should be avoided.

❖ Previous research has used case studies to develop understanding of how HRM affects individual performance by researching organisations that had achieved high-performance outcomes (Truss, 2001). We therefore used a multiple case study approach (Eisenhardt, 1989) for this research.

WHO WE GATHERED THE DATA FROM

This section summarises the key characteristics of the individuals who participated in this research, in order to demonstrate the spread of organisations, job types and levels of those taking part.

Interviews

We conducted three types of interview:

❖ Access interviews – intended to gather contextual and background data specific to each case site organisation and held mainly with directors of the organisation concerned.

❖ Employee interviews – the majority of our sample (172 interviews) – intended to obtain individual perspectives on how HRM influences performance. These interviews comprised a series of questions (see Appendix 1) and a card-sort to explore the way in which individuals thought that various HR practices related to each other and impacted on their own performance.

LIVERPOOL JOHN MOORES UNIVERSITY
LEARNING SERVICES

❖ Interviews with staff from partner and contractor organisations – intended to develop understanding of partnership and contracting arrangements in practice.

In total, 218 interviews were conducted. (The breakdown by interview type is shown in Table 2 on page 8.) We used data from these interviews in various elements of the analysis; this is described in more detail in the relevant chapters of this report.

Individuals from a range of professions were interviewed. The categories used to describe NHS staff job types (see www.ic.nhs.uk/statistics-and-data-collections/workforce/nhs-staff-numbers) were used as a basis for analysis, although we did separate out HR professionals because of the focus of the research (see Table 4 below).

Table 2 ❖ Total interview numbers per case site

Site	Access interviews	Employee interviews	Partner/contractor interviews
1	3	32	7
2	3	27	2
3	3	28	2
4	4	29	7
5	5	22	2
6	6	30	10
Total	24	168	30

Note: Partner and contractor interviews and analysis focused on sites 1, 4 and 6. Some of these interviews (14) were with senior managers within the Trust, and replicate interviews classified as either Access or Employee.

Table 4 ❖ Employee interviews by job type

Job type	Employee interviews	%
Directors	20	12
HR professionals	20	12
Clinical staff	55	33
Support workers	17	10
Admin and clerical	42	25
Hotel and estates	12	7
Union representatives	2	1

Note: 'Union representatives' only refers to those with a full-time union role.

Individuals from a range of organisational levels took part in employee interviews. The NHS has a national pay system – Agenda for Change (AfC) (for details see www.dh.gov.uk/en/Policyandguidance/Humanresourcesandtraining/Modernisingpay/Agendaforchange/index.htm) for all staff apart from very senior managers (normally directors), doctors and dentists, which was used to categorise individuals (Table 3 below). We did not aim to replicate national profiles in terms of the proportion of individuals from each pay band, but rather to include a cross-section of individual job types and organisational levels within each case study organisation.

The individuals were selected at random by administrative staff within the case study organisation and covered a range of directorates within the organisation. Some key characteristics of the individuals are shown in Table 5.

Table 3 ❖ Employee interviews by pay band

Pay band	Employee interviews	%
1–4	59	35
5–7	51	30
8	29	17
Director	20	12
Doctor	9	6

Table 5 ❖ Gender distribution, NHS and Trust tenure

	%
Gender distribution	
Female	62
Male	38
NHS tenure	
Under 6 years	32
6 to 15 years	14
16 years and over	54
Trust tenure	
Under 6 years	63
6 to 15 years	10
16 years and over	27

Workshops

Senior HR managers (45) from a variety of NHS organisations were involved in workshops at which the preliminary findings from the empirical research were presented. These workshops offered valuable insights into current HRM practice, and stimulated and refined the ideas that are described in this report. We offer our sincere thanks to all of those who contributed.

WHERE DIFFERENCES BETWEEN ORGANISATIONS AND INDIVIDUALS ARE IMPORTANT

Throughout this report we refer to differences between data gathered from each case study organisation and from individuals only where it was shown to be important. The three types of NHS organisation – acute, mental health, and primary care – were more similar to each other than might have been expected; the differences were more marked between individual case study organisations than between types of organisation. Similarly, there were differences in the findings from some elements of the research depending on the type of job held by individuals, or the level of the organisation, but there were fewer differences than might have been expected. These issues are therefore mentioned only when it is of importance to the overall point being made.

HOW DATA IS PRESENTED

We use quotes throughout this report to illustrate points that are being made. We have been very careful in our analysis of the data (see Appendix 1) to ensure that the points made are drawn robustly from the evidence gathered, and at no point do we draw conclusions from comments made by a single individual.

REPORT STRUCTURE

The report is structured around the framework we have developed to analyse the data. This is described in Chapter 2 but summarised here.

Chapter 3 describes the case study organisations
It describes the case study organisations in terms of their organisational strategy, HRM strategy and HRM content. This section illustrates the different arrangements for HRM in participating organisations.

Chapters 4 to 6 analyse various elements of the HRM systems including contracting and partnership
Chapter 4 examines how key strategic decisions – such as whether to contract out services, to work in partnership or to maintain in-house provision – operate in practice and how they can affect patient care. It identifies the potential gains from and obstacles to effective contracting and partnership working.

Chapter 5 assesses individual perceptions of HRM and how individuals understand the HR practices used within the organisation.

Chapter 6 illustrates how line managers play a critical role in bringing HR practices to life, and analyses the constraints and enablers to effective HRM delivery through line managers.

Chapter 7 and 8 relate to the psychological contract in NHS organisations
Chapter 7 illustrates components of the psychological contract in healthcare by analysing the expectations of those who work in healthcare, and the extent to which these expectations are fulfilled.

Chapter 8 explores what individuals believe their employers expect of them, and gives examples of individuals going beyond expectations.

Chapter 9 describes individual and organisational performance
This chapter illustrates individual perceptions/conceptions of performance at both individual and organisational level. It also explores the links between these levels.

Chapter 10 concludes the report and indicates the implications of the findings
The report concludes by highlighting the processes of HRM engagement and alignment, and how these might be achieved. It also presents implications for national policy-makers, healthcare organisations and HR professionals.

HOW TO USE THIS REPORT

Each chapter that describes empirical data (Chapters 3 to 9) starts with a summary of its key conclusions and a diagram to show how it fits with the overall framework for the research. A common structure for each chapter is then used:

❖ What does this chapter cover?

❖ What is the context?

❖ Why is this important?

❖ Where did the data come from?

❖ What was found?

❖ Conclusions?

❖ What are the links with the rest of the research?

❖ Learning points – for the organisation and the HRM system/HR function

Different readers will have different requirements and so we have highlighted below the various elements that might interest individual readers, depending on their perspective.

If you are very short of time ...
Read the executive summary for the main conclusions and implications for organisations and the HR function.

If you are in a hurry but have some time ...
Read the Executive summary and the learning points from each chapter (which are then summarised in Chapter 10).

If you have time to read two chapters ...
Read Chapter 1 and Chapter 10 which set the scene and summarise the findings and implications.

If you are interested in how the findings are supported by other research ...
Read Chapter 2 which gives examples of other research that has explored the links between HRM and performance. Hyde *et al* (2006a and 2006b) provide a full literature review. Throughout this report there are boxes headed *Is this supported by other research?* which indicate comparisons between these findings and other research.

If you are an HR professional and want to know what we found out about HRM ...
Read Chapter 4, *HRM strategy: working with other organisations*, Chapter 5, *HR content: understanding, practices and perceptions* and Chapter 6, *HR content: the role of line managers*. The theoretical basis for the concept of the HRM system can be found in Chapter 2. Implications for the HR function are summarised in Chapter 10.

If you want to know what we found out about individuals and their psychological contracts ...
Read Chapter 7, *Individuals: their expectations of work* and Chapter 8, *Individuals: perceptions of employer expectations*.

If you want to know what we found out about performance ...
Read Chapter 9, *Performance in the NHS: individuals and organisations*.

If you are an HR professional and want to know what the implications are for you ...
Read the Executive summary or Chapter 10, *Conclusions*, which gives further detail.

If you are a board member or senior manager ...
Any of the findings may be of interest, but if time is short, focus on Chapter 9: *Performance in the NHS: individuals and organisations*, and the implications for organisations in Chapter 10.

HRM AND PERFORMANCE – UNDERSTANDING THE RELATIONSHIP

2

❖ **It is not always easy to describe organisational strategy in the NHS, although a clear strategy does enable priorities for each area of the organisation to be established.**

❖ **The HRM system comprises *HRM strategy* and *HR content*, which includes HR practices.**

❖ **The HRM–performance link is a process, with various events occurring over time.**

WHAT DOES THIS CHAPTER COVER?

This chapter explains the theoretical basis for the research and the various concepts that are used. It shows how the detailed results which follow (Chapters 3 to 9) support the overall framework for the research.

Terminology:
Throughout this report, 'HR' refers to the specialist HR function and 'HRM' is the generic term for the management of people throughout the organisation, unless indicated otherwise.

INTRODUCTION

The basic elements of the research were shown in Figure 1, and we explained in Chapter 1 how we understand 'HRM' to mean the HRM system – both HRM strategy and content, the individual perspective to be described in terms of the psychological contract, and performance to comprise both individual and organisation performance. The first phase of this research (Hyde *et al*, 2006a) showed that there was a need for a deeper understanding of how HRM related to performance, and that exploration of the role of the individual in this would be one way of doing this.

In this chapter we detail these elements and describe them within the context of the NHS. We also demonstrate how they relate to each other, using a process framework which recognises the influence of external factors on the relationship between HRM and performance at all stages, as well as the links between organisational and HRM strategy (Bowen and Ostroff, 2004).

Why we have used a process model

The model we have developed is shown in Figure 3 on page 12. It was developed after our thinking was stimulated by the model proposed by Boselie *et al* (2005), who questioned the smooth sequential process linking HRM to performance outcomes assumed in earlier empirical research. They suggested (p.78) that rather than being a uni-directional process, each factor interacts with the next.

> *The mere presence of such practices is unlikely to be sufficient. The quality of implementation, in terms of effectiveness, procedural justice etc – is a vital determinant of the success or otherwise of an organisation's HRM performance.*

The remainder of this chapter summarises the elements of this model and signposts where in this report the detailed evidence for each of these elements can be found.

ORGANISATIONAL STRATEGY

An organisational strategy sets out the stated aims of an organisation, normally in the form of a vision statement or a 'big idea' (Purcell *et al*, 2003) and the means by which these aims are to be achieved. Contextual issues are interpreted differently in each organisation, depending on its stage of development and the needs of its own local population. It can be argued that *what* NHS organisations do is open to little debate and local focus, but *how* they deliver healthcare is the key thing that may distinguish them from other providers. An 'organisational strategy' is not always easy to identify within NHS organisations – not least because the terminology may be different, eg, 'service development strategy'.

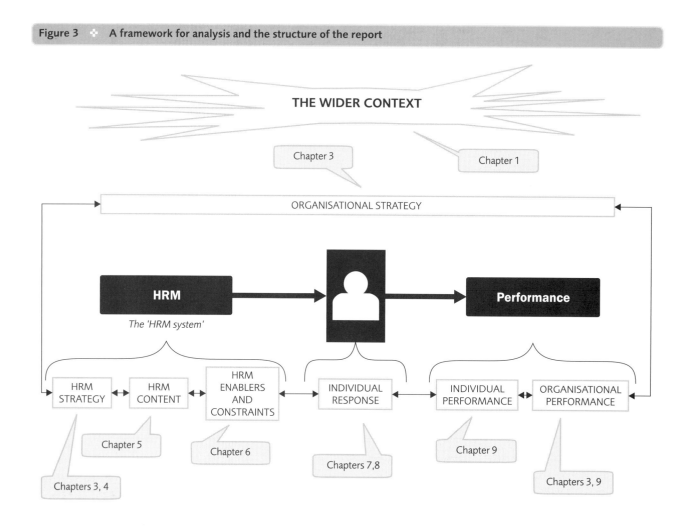

Figure 3 ❖ **A framework for analysis and the structure of the report**

Why does organisational strategy matter?

It is argued (Vere, 2005; p.xi) that public sector organisations require a sufficiently well developed business strategy to enable HRM priorities to be identified and that HR should work in partnership with senior managers in developing strategy:

> Strategic HR capability means understanding the business and establishing productive relationships with managers across the organisation.

Organisational strategy at each case study organisation is summarised in Chapter 3.

THE HRM SYSTEM

The HRM system (Bowen and Ostroff, 2004) comprises both the *HRM strategy* for the organisation and the *HR content –* specific HR polices and practices. It integrates content (individual practices and policies intended to achieve particular strategic objectives) and process (design and administration intended to form shared understanding of the content). In this research we describe the process in terms of enablers and constraints for HRM.

HRM strategy

HRM strategy translates organisational strategy and the features of the wider context into a workforce strategy which includes systems for delivering HRM, strategic decisions about employment relationships, and sets of HR practices and policies. It also involves being concerned with both content and process of HRM delivery. In the healthcare sector, an increasing number of staff are employed by organisations other than the NHS, and it is likely that these organisations will have different aims and objectives that may or may not conflict with those of NHS Trusts. Effective delivery of patient care is therefore complicated because control and responsibility extends across organisational boundaries, and it cannot be assumed that synergies will flow automatically from contracting and partnership-working or that these will be desired. Much depends on the way in which these relationships are established and the grounds on which they are based (Marchington *et al*, 2005).

HRM strategy at the case sites, including the approach taken to partnership and outsourcing, is outlined and assessed in Chapters 3 and 4.

The effects of contracting out and forming partnerships are analysed in Chapter 4.

HRM strategy in the NHS as a whole

Changes to the NHS workforce have been numerous over the past few years as a result of policy changes as well as other contextual factors. Some policies have been described as HR strategies whereas others have had indirect but significant influence on workforce issues. An excellent summary can be found in Chapter 2 of the House of Commons Health Committee report on Workforce Planning (House of Commons Health Committee, 2007). Some of the key elements relevant to this research include:

April 2000 – DH paper *A Health Service of All the Talents* published

July 2000 – publication of the NHS Plan; start of Improving Working Lives scheme

July 2002 – *HR in the NHS Plan* published: structured around four pillars of activity to enable the recruitment and retention of more staff and the redesign of jobs around the patient:

❖ *model employer* – making the NHS a model employer by creating an environment for healthy work–life balance, a diverse workforce, job security, fair pay, lifelong learning and staff involvement and partnership working. Measured through Improving Working Lives target

❖ *model careers* – providing model careers through the 'skills escalator', pay modernisation, learning and personal development, professional regulation and workforce planning

❖ *staff morale* – recognising that staff attitudes and behaviours impact on patient care, and

❖ *building people management skills* – through leadership development and national HR networks.

April 2003 – new consultant contract begins

April 2004 – new GP contract begins

August 2004 – European Working Time Directive extended to trainee doctors

December 2004 – *Agenda for Change* agreement finalised

April 2005 – new pharmacy services contract begins: NHS deficit in excess of £250 million

November 2005 – Secretary of State commits to achieving net NHS financial balance by end of 2006/7

December 2005 – *A national framework to support local workforce strategy development: A guide for HR directors in the NHS and social care* published, allowing organisations the autonomy to develop their own HRM systems to fit their local environment, moving policy away from standardised HRM and towards locally tailored approaches (Marchington and Grugulis, 2000). It emphasises the need for a 'clear line of sight between HR practices and the delivery of high-quality services' (DH, 2005; p.3) and highlights four key HR practices:

❖ high-impact HR: 10 high-impact HR changes that can 'improve organisational efficiency and improve quality and the patient experience' (pp50–1)

❖ model employer

❖ skills escalator

❖ integrated planning.

January 2006 – publication of *Our Health, Our Care, Our Say* White Paper proposing plans to shift hospital activity into primary care

April 2006 – new dentistry contract begins: NHS deficit reaches £547 million.

DOES RESEARCH SHOW THAT HRM STRATEGY MATTERS?

Examples of supporting research include:

❖ HRM assets and liabilities were identified as one of five core factors for successful organisational change (Pettigrew and Whipp, 1991).

❖ A literature review of influences on various performance measures (improvement) within public services (Boyne, 2003) showed that 'resources' and 'management' (leadership style and expertise, organisational culture, HRM and strategy process and content) are the two most consistent influences on performance. The method used for review was not dissimilar to the literature review which formed the first phase of this research (Hyde *et al*, 2006).

HR content

The content of HR relates to specific HR policies and practices. It has to be aligned with other key systems and management processes inside the organisation (Hendry *et al*, 1989; Pettigrew *et al*, 1992).

HRM AND PERFORMANCE – UNDERSTANDING THE RELATIONSHIP

In this research we have used 11 HR practices that we derived from an analysis of the literature (Purcell *et al*, 2003), the first report from this research (Hyde *et al*, 2006a), and a series of focus groups (see Appendix 1) and include:

❖ appraisal

❖ career development

❖ communication (ie between management and individuals)

❖ employee involvement (ie involvement in decisions)

❖ job security

❖ pay

❖ recruitment

❖ rewards (ie non-monetary rewards)

❖ teamworking

❖ training

❖ work–life balance.

HR content as perceived by individuals at each case study organisation is described in Chapter 5.

DOES RESEARCH SHOW THAT HR CONTENT MATTERS?

Examples of research that shows this include:

❖ Sophistication of appraisal has been linked to reduced patient mortality, as has sophistication of training and percentage of staff working in teams (West *et al*, 2002).

❖ A further study suggested that 'high-involvement' HRM policies (training, performance management, participation, decentralisation, employee involvement, use of teams, employment security and Investor in People status) may contribute to high-quality health care (West *et al*, 2006).

❖ Recent studies, largely in the private sector, have found associations between sets of HR practices called high-performance work practices (HPWPs) and improved organisational performance (Combs *et al*, 2006; p.524):

Our results lay to rest any doubts about the existence of a relationship ... We estimate that organisations can increase their performance by 0.20 of a standardised unit for each unit increase in HPWP used.

Table 6 ❖ HR high-impact changes	
The change	**Related HR practice**
1 Support and lead effective change management	❖ Communication (ie between managment and individuals) ❖ Employee involvement (ie involvement in decisions)
2 Develop effective recruitment, good induction and supportive management	❖ Recruitment
3 Develop shared service models and effective use of IT	
4 Manage temporary staffing costs	❖ Job security
5 Promote staff health and manage sickness absence	❖ Work–life balance
6 Promote job and service redesign	❖ Teamworking
7 Develop and implement appraisal	❖ Appraisal
8 Involve staff and work in partnership to develop good employee relations	❖ Communication (ie between management and individuals) ❖ Employee involvement (ie involvement in decisions)
9 Champion good people management practices	All practices could be included in this
10 Provide effective training and development	❖ Training

HR content in the NHS and the HR high-impact changes

In 2006 the NHS promoted ten high-impact HR changes that can 'improve organisational efficiency and improve quality and the patient experience' (DH 2006a; pp50–1). These relate in many cases directly to HR practices (Table 6 on page 14).

HRM ENABLERS AND CONSTRAINTS

Many studies (eg Boselie *et al*, 2005) suggest that it is not enough to have particular HR practices in place: the potential impact of any HR practice or set of practices may be mediated by the effect of the implementation process on individuals and thus on HRM outcomes such as motivation, commitment and satisfaction. However, except for a small number of notable exceptions, there is little information about *how* HRM affects individual performance (see for examples Purcell *et al*, 2003; Guest and Conway, 2004). The way in which individuals perceive HR content and the extent to which it aligns with the overall organisational strategy and the design of the HRM systems, is important (Hodgkinson and Sparrow, 2002).

Chapter 5 analyses individual perceptions of HR practices.

Line managers are recognised as crucial in bringing HR practices to life. Alongside devolution of responsibilities for HRM, it is partnership between HR professionals and line managers that is a critical factor that helps to explain the impact of HRM initiatives (Whittaker and Marchington, 2003). The involvement of line managers in bringing HR policies to life has been demonstrated as important in generating performance effects from high-performance practices (Purcell *et al*, 2003).

Chapter 6 examines the role of line managers.

THE INDIVIDUAL

We use the concept of the psychological contract between employers and employees (Rousseau, 2001) to explore individual perceptions of the relationship between HRM and performance. Explanations can be made of specific aspects of the linkage between HRM and performance such as theories of cognitive processes (Wright and Haggerty, 2005) which may help to explain the individual processes and performance outcomes that are triggered by HRM systems. Individuals develop a number of necessary emotional and attitudinal states – for example, perceptions of trust, fairness, perceived organisational support, and confidence in the relationship they have with managers. These states act as precursors to a healthy psychological contract. As a product of the exchange relationship at work (the psychological contract) a number of attitudes – such as commitment to the organisation and engagement with its goals necessary for the delivery of performance – can then be developed.

The employee–employer relationship is an essential component of HRM (Sparrow and Cooper 2003). The importance of the psychological contract has been noted in the NHS, in that the NHS is perceived as a good employer having made more promises and commitments to employees, which were linked to higher levels of satisfaction, commitment, excitement, loyalty to clients, motivation and less intention to leave (Guest and Conway, 2004).

Chapters 7 and 8 illustrate the psychological contract in the case study organisations.

PERFORMANCE

In this research, performance has been considered at both the individual and the organisational level. The distinction between performance in terms of the process of care provision, as distinct from the outcomes of healthcare provision for the patient, has also been considered.

Individual performance contributes to organisational performance, and these dynamics will be presented here. This research is not concerned with performance measurement systems or the process of performance management within organisations, but rather on how performance is understood and the influences on it.

Chapter 3 provides objective data about organisational performance in the case study organisations.

Chapter 9 analyses perceptions of individual and organisational performance in the case study organisations.

How is HRM linked to performance within healthcare?

There is a wide range of research on this subject (see Hyde *et al*, 2006a) little of which is specific to healthcare. Additionally, Flood (1994) notes that relating organisational factors (ie HRM structure) directly to outcomes is dangerous – it can bypass an understanding of the process by which structure affects outcomes – which is the focus of this research.

Previous studies linking structure in terms of HRM to outcome (eg West *et al*, 2002) acknowledge this as a limitation of their work (West *et al*, 2002; p.1309):

> ... more research is needed carefully to examine the underlying mechanisms responsible for these associations.

Subsequent work (West *et al*, 2006; p.997) suggests

> a number of important and intriguing theoretical questions arising from our research. The most obvious is to identify the mechanisms mediating the relationship between the HRM system variables and patient mortality more precisely ...

RELATIONSHIPS BETWEEN THE ELEMENTS OF THE FRAMEWORK

Individual elements of the research demonstrate *what* is involved in HRM influencing performance. However, to demonstrate *how* HRM can influence performance, it is necessary to understand the relationship between these elements. We will show that there are three aspects to how HRM influences performance: a *process* of *engagement* and *alignment*.

Process: the relationship between HRM and performance as a process

There are various elements of process theory (Buchanan *et al*, 2007) that may contribute, but here we focus on

❖ cumulative effects – where outcomes depend on an accumulation of factors, so that no single factor is responsible for the outcome (Pierson, 2003)

❖ path dependency – where the outcomes are shaped by earlier circumstances and critical events during the process. This approach explores incidents which trigger patterns of action, the decisions of key individuals over time and patterns of response to those decisions. It leads to the conclusion that if similar sequences of events are observed in different settings, 'inferences can be drawn concerning how these conditions, in this kind of context, can trigger this event sequence, producing those outcomes' (Buchanan *et al*, 2007; p.239). Boxall and Purcell (2003) argue that path dependency is a key element in our understanding of how HRM works within and between organisations.

Where possible we have also identified enablers to and constraints on the various elements of the process.

Alignment of each stage of the process

This is another concept which we have developed through this research, although it does build on existing theories.

❖ There must be alignment between organisational goals and individual expectations. Recognition of the need for such alignment is especially important during organisational change.

❖ In the description of a strong HRM system by Bowen and Ostroff (2004), one of the factors affecting it is described as 'consistency' – establishing an effect over time. This involves instrumentality (unambiguous cause–effect relationship influenced by employee perceptions) and

consistent HRM messages (espoused and inferred values) – for example, where teamwork is required, it is teams that are rewarded.

❖ There are also models of alignment between various levels of the organisation (Fiol *et al*, 2001) which can be used to aid understanding of alignment between individuals and the organisation.

❖ There are other perspectives on alignment which may be important but are not a key focus of this research. These include alignment with community needs (NHS Confederation, 2007a; p.11):

a responsibility to ... the wider community ... how [healthcare organisations] connect to the community becomes a question for constant review. To identify unmet needs and anticipate changing patterns of use is key to how they set up their services.

Engagement: the HRM system engaging with each element of the process

This is a concept which we have developed through this research. We suggest that there are three directions for HRM engagement:

❖ engagement in influencing and developing organisational strategy and translating policy into local actions – This may also involve flexibility in terms of HR practices and policies to accommodate different situations and individual circumstances. *The HRM role in this context is one of translation and adaptation.*

❖ engagement with different parts of the organisation and partner organisations: directorates and professional groups – *The HRM role in this context is one of communication.*

❖ engagement with individuals delivering services, including the organisation's workforce as well as those employed by other agencies – *The HRM role in this context is one of understanding.*

CONCLUSION

This chapter shows that there are various elements to the HRM–performance relationship, and that these can be linked through a process of engagement and alignment. Subsequent chapters describe and analyse the data which led us to develop this model, Chapter 10 draws together the findings into this model and summarises learning points and implications for practice.

HRM AND PERFORMANCE – THE CASE STUDY ORGANISATIONS

❖ **Six case study organisations were used in this research: two Acute, two Mental Health and two Primary Care Trusts.**

❖ **Each organisation had developed its own organisational and HRM strategies in response to the wider context and local circumstances. There was little commonality in terms of organisational or HRM strategy content between the various types of organisation – eg Acute Trusts.**

❖ **National performance data does not give detailed insight into the differences between each of the case study organisations, or give insight into the HRM systems within the organisations.**

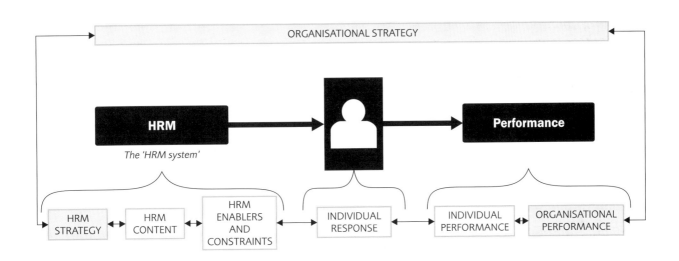

WHAT DOES THIS CHAPTER COVER?

This chapter describes each case study organisation in brief. It provides

❖ a summary of organisational strategies and the impact of the context on the organisation

❖ HRM structures and strategy – details of the HR function, HRM strategy and types of HR practices adopted at each case study site

❖ HR content – brief outlines of the priorities in HR practices at each case study site

❖ performance histories – star ratings, annual health check, staff and patient satisfaction survey results.

ORGANISATIONAL HISTORY AND CURRENT STRATEGY

A brief summary of the key elements of the organisational history of each case study organisation is given in Table 7 on page 18. The following three examples show how Trust strategy was used.

1 Foundation status seen as a means of closer involvement with the community

This was evident at both Cases 3 and 4:

Everyone at the Trust is really excited about the opportunities being an NHS Foundation Trust will bring. We have a real track record of involving and engaging our service users, their carers, local people,

Table 7 ❖ Case study organisations	
Case 1	This Acute Trust was formed in 2001 after a merger with two local acute trusts. Community, primary care and therapy services were then split off to the PCT in April 2002. It operates from four sites, the main one being a District General Hospital; the three smaller sites focus on diagnostics, orthopaedics and sub-acute care within a separate out-patient centre.
Case 2	This Acute Trust has recently undergone a major re-development programme, funded through the Private Finance Initiative (PFI) involving building and relocating its main headquarters and hospital site, and also relocating other services to this site. The PFI is a partnership between the Trust and three healthcare private sector groups and provides all non-clinical support at the hospital for the next 40 years The new development was opened in 2005 and there is now a single in-patient hospital site and two other out-patient centres.
Case 3	This Mental Health Trust achieved Foundation status in May 2006. It provides a wide range of mental health (MH) services including neuro-developmental, learning disability, forensic MH, specialist care for children, eating disorders and substance misuse. The Trust also provides a range of services for the four PCTs in its area on a shared services basis. Clinical services are delivered across 71 premises.
Case 4	This partnership Mental Health Trust achieved Foundation status in May 2006. It was formed in 2002 following agreement to enter full partnership agreements with three local councils. It provides health and social care services for people with mental health problems and learning disabilities. The Trust also delivers forensic mental health services.
Case 5	This PCT was first formed in 2002 through the merger of five healthcare organisations including a former Community Trust and two Primary Care Groups. An internal reorganisation took place in January 2006, merging two directorates so that there are now five. Further internal reorganisation took place in October 2006 to reflect the separation of commissioning and provider functions following the publication of *Commissioning a Patient-Led NHS* (DH, 2006b).
Case 6	This PCT was established in 2002 and is in an area of significant deprivation. The Chief Executive appointed at that time also remained Director of Social Services of the local council, which led the way for further joint appointments across the PCT and social services. It describes itself as having a 'very close relationship with the council's Social Services Department and with the wider local authority' (Trust website), including 'pooled budgets, integrated management arrangements and, increasingly, services' through the establishment of a formal partnership arrangement with the local authority in 2005/6.

our partners and our staff, and as an NHS Foundation Trust we can take this even further – we are on the verge of something really special here. Mental health, learning disability and children's services in — have been judged to be some of the best in the country, and we should all be proud of this achievement.

(Director)

I see this as a major step forward as I have now at the moment X thousand members and that's X thousand champions in the community. I've just appointed Y governors, so we are really now starting, we're really involving the community – even though we've always involved them – but I think now involving them in a more meaningful way and giving them power ... Membership [is] made up of service users, carers, staff, business communities, local politicians.

(Director)

2 Developing clear links between elements of the organisational strategy

Case 4 used the opportunity to apply for Foundation status to review its strategic direction. As a result:

... This helped us make those connections [between service development strategy, HR strategy and workforce plan] much, much stronger. You will not see anything now in any of our plans that doesn't link with the service development strategy. We have got to be absolutely sure that every activity within this organisation supports the business, and we are clear about that – and that is quite a fundamental change.

(Director)

The way in which these are linked is shown in Figure 4 opposite.

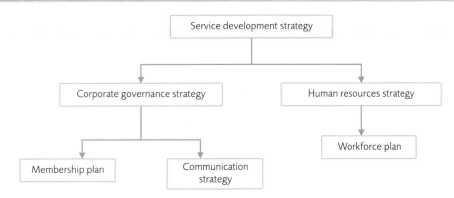

Figure 4 ❖ Strategy structure at Case 4

3 A long-term strategy communicated to all

Case 6's aim was 'integrating to improve services', leading to fully integrated service provision in 2010, and at the time of the research was four years into an eight-year plan to provide services in this way. Key points from the plan were printed on all staff diaries with associated HR policies and developments. For example, 2006/7 was the 'year of opportunity and investment' (see Table 8), which included investing in services that demonstrated targeted improvement to narrow the gap in health inequality and reduced reliance on hospital services.

Table 8 ❖ Strategic staircase goals for the years 2002 to 2010 at Case 6

Year	Purpose
2002/3	A year of design
2003/4	A year of building
2004/5	A year of delivery
2005/6	Year of engagement and involvement
2006/7	Year of opportunity and investment
2007/8	Year of transformation
2008/9	Year of empowerment and culture
2009/10	Year of excellence

Source: staff handbook and diary 2006/7

Each case study organisation had a mission or values statement which is shown in Table 9 on page 20. Although all of these mention the patient, or community, the focus varies:

❖ Both Acute Trusts include a statement about *patient* needs that reflects the focus of the acute sector on treating illness.

❖ The two Mental Health Trusts focus on *partnership* in service provision, which reflects the complex needs of patients who require mental health services.

❖ The two PCTs focus on improving the health of the *community*, highlighting the role of primary care in preventing ill-health.

HRM strategy

All case study organisations had some form of strategy described as 'HR' which emphasised various elements. Examples are given below.

The role of HRM in improving patient care

At Case 1 the HR strategy had two main targets:

❖ achieving workforce characteristics – a workforce that has the 'essential skills, knowledge, and attitudes'

❖ a positive working environment – to enable staff to maximise their contribution.

The Trust believed that it was essential to provide equal attention to both targets, and that by doing so it provided the best possible patient services.

At Case 2 the HR strategy stated that HR was there to 'Make it easier for our organisation and workforce to deliver fantastic results'. This was then summarised as

Promoting what does work, challenging what doesn't work, and stimulating change, in order to ensure that our patients receive the best care that our workforce can provide and they don't feel let down by the service we provide.

Table 9 ✣ Mission and vision statements	
Case 1: mission statement	To create the right conditions for our staff to put our patients' needs at the heart of everything we do
Case 2: vision	To be the hospital of choice for local people, providing high-quality healthcare services, which respond to patients' needs
Case 3: purpose	To provide the local and wider communities with the best range of integrated care for adults and children, including specialised mental health and learning disability services and community teams. We achieve this through creating partnerships and a culture of development and continuous improvement and keeping the patient at the centre of everything we do
Case 4: mission statement	To work in partnership to provide innovative leading-edge care services for our community which promote recovery and well-being, maximise individual choice and enable people to live as independently as possible
Case 5: mission statement	To improve the health and well-being of the community, particularly members of the community who experience disadvantage
Case 6: vision	The local communities we serve will be more informed about their health, involved in decisions that affect it, and experience better health and well-being and improved health and social care services

The role of HRM in developing the workforce

Trusts were also clear that there should be a focus on the workforce themselves, and the environment in which they work.

The HR strategy at Case 3 aspired to

have people delivering excellent services – right values, right skills, right numbers, diverse backgrounds and is representative of the community.

One of the stated organisational values at Case 6 was

commitment to be a good employer, demonstrating our commitment to staff development, involving and engaging the workforce and striving to make X a place where people want to live and work.

The integration of HRM strategy with organisational strategy

This was explicit at Case 4 (see Figure 4 on page 19).

We need to recruit, retain and develop excellent people by ensuring that all people policies, practices and initiatives integrate with and underpin the service development strategy and strategic objectives in order to deliver excellent productive services.

(Director)

Such integration is not only about strategy but about how it is implemented and monitored.

The HR strategy at Case 4 was clear there had to be

✣ *recognition at board level that the way in which HR is performed is synonymous with the culture of the Trust*

✣ *regular checks and reports from external and internal auditors*

✣ *Director of HR on the Audit Committee*

✣ *HR user groups*

✣ *regular feedback on HR issues from the Joint Staff Forum*

✣ *HR and IWL Steering Group which consists of a selection of staff at various levels and staff representatives, and includes an infrastructure of subcommittees covering areas such as equality and diversity and policy development, that report back to it.*

At Case 6 the HR strategy was translated into service objectives and monitored quarterly on an internal basis.

The HRM strategy at most case study organisations included elements of national HR frameworks – eg the four pillars of a model employer – as might be expected. There was evidence of adding to these for local focus.

Developing the HRM strategy in partnership with employees/trade unions

Some case study organisations were explicit about the way in which HRM strategy was developed:

> *...If we are developing something as critical as an HR strategy, it is almost second nature that engagement and consultation would be part of that ... Staff side were part of our steering group in producing that strategy, so they were absolutely signed up and could use their mechanisms.*

(Director)

It should be noted that Case 5 was developing a new HR strategy during the period of research so it was not possible to use it in this analysis.

THE STRUCTURE OF THE HR FUNCTION

HR structures varied across Cases (see Table 10 below). For example, Cases 3, 4 and 5 had HR advisers/managers attached to services and directorates. At Case 6 HR was centralised and shared some aspects of HR provision with the local authority. All had an HR director on the board, although some were also responsible for other areas of activity in addition to HR.

AGENDA FOR CHANGE (AfC)

AfC is a new pay and reward system applying to all directly employed NHS staff except very senior managers and doctors. It was agreed with the NHS unions in November 2004 and rolled out from December 2004, with the aim of 100% assimilation (apart from those who wished to remain on local contracts) by 30 September 2005. It was intended to ensure fair pay and a clearer system for career progression. Staff are now paid on the basis of the jobs they are doing and the skills and knowledge they apply to these jobs, underpinned by a job evaluation scheme specifically designed for the NHS.

These changes occurred during the period of this research when the experience of the process of assimilation to new pay bands was still fresh in the minds of many individuals, as quotes and comments in this report show.

HR CONTENT

In line with the NHS as a whole, the HR policies and practices at each case site were shaped significantly by national policies, and in broad terms they had much in common. Nevertheless, there were differences between the cases depending on a variety of factors:

Table 10	HR structures at the case study sites

	HR director background	Structure of HR function	Organisation of HR
1 **Acute**	In post since formation of Trust (2001)	Training and development team and HR function in the HR departments, with HR staff dedicated 'virtually' to one or more operating divisions	Centralised service
2 **Acute**	NHS background since 1995	Merged management structure	Advisers attached to directorates
3 **MH**	In post since formation of Trust (2002)	Directorate of HR and OD split in two, both teams being housed in the same building	Advisers attached to directorates
4 **MH**	Clinical – four years in HR	Workforce and Business Development split into Workforce Development and Training and Human Resources	Advisers attached to directorates
5 **PCT**	HR in retail and local authority	Director of HR and OD plus Head of HR. Covers learning/development, recruitment, HR management, workforce information	Managers attached to directorates
6 **PCT**	Public sector HR	Integrated Health and Social Case directorate, comprising general resourcing and workforce development	Centralised service for HR advice and guidance

❖ local contingencies (eg having to pay higher rates of pay in certain areas due to intense labour market competition)

❖ identified weaknesses in the organisation (eg poor results in the staff satisfaction survey)

❖ the preferences of senior management (eg those components of HRM which were given priority within the organisation).

This led them to prioritise some HR practices over others, and to place greater emphasis on developing and reinforcing these practices as part of the drive to create a 'stronger' HRM system. Data from the access interviews and those with senior managers at each of the case sites were examined in order to identify which practices were deemed most important and why. These are presented below.

Involvement and communications

At Case 1 the value of employee involvement and communications, and the need to develop it further, was stressed by several directors. This was seen as a key management philosophy in relation to all staff but also as a specific form of collaboration with the staff side representatives via local partnership arrangements. One director believed this was a true partnership in that opportunities were provided for joint working in order to identify areas for improvement, and there was a communications sub-group whose job it was to enhance existing forms of dialogue. Results from the staff satisfaction survey showed Case 1 as above-average in terms of job satisfaction and feedback from managers to staff, but also in the top 20% for the coverage and effectiveness of appraisals (see Figure 7 on page 25), demonstrating the effectiveness of employee involvement.

Change having an impact on staff satisfaction

Case 2, the other Acute Trust, received somewhat poorer ratings from the staff satisfaction survey, coming in the lowest 20% for appraisal and feedback, and for job satisfaction. Not surprisingly, perhaps, the main focus at Case 2 – according to several directors – was on rolling out a new performance management system, although it was recognised that recent changes (including the introduction of a PFI) had destabilised things, which was perhaps reflected in the staff survey results. The appraisal system that was being implemented clearly linked individual performance to that of the Trust as a whole. One director felt that the organisation operated with an open-door policy – something that came across in the interviews undertaken with staff at Case 2. The other new initiative that was about to be implemented was on team-based working, derived from the Aston University model and research.

Involvement and communication supported by training

Case 3 is a Mental Health Trust in which the senior managers reported that they also prioritised employee involvement, communications and teamworking. The employee involvement framework used here had been developed through focus groups with staff, the results of a staff opinion survey and talking with trade unions on the staff side. This was another Trust to use external academic support – in this case to develop team-work across the organisation. A third key component of the approach at Case 3 was a substantial investment in training for 120 middle and senior managers in preparation for moves to Foundation Trust status. Staff attitudes at this case study were very positive indeed (see Figure 7); the trust is among the top 20% for most categories.

The impact of communication

The other Mental Health Trust, Case 4, also appeared to focus on similar HR practices – namely, communications and training. The former was one of the most visible and important aspects of HRM that the Trust was engaged in. In practice this took a number of forms, such as a staff intranet, regular meetings between the CEO and small groups of staff from across the Trust, and close working between management and the staff side in developing the long-term strategy of the organisation. This appeared to achieve fruition given the results of the staff survey (see Figure 7): Case 4 was among the top 20% of all Mental Health Trusts in just about every category relating to staff satisfaction, feedback from managers and the coverage and effectiveness of the appraisal system. As with Case 3, there had been an emphasis on management training recently, in particular in helping managers – especially those new to the role – to learn how to deal with HR issues. This is not to say that this Trust faced no problems, of course, and one of the major issues was how to reward people effectively in an environment in which many other – often better-paying – jobs were available.

Prioritising performance management, communication and teamworking

At Case 5, a PCT, results from the staff survey were rather less positive than at Case 4, the scores for a number of areas (eg appraisal and job satisfaction) either average or below average (see Figure 7). On appraisal one director was fully aware that things needed to improve, and this may be why there was a strong emphasis in access interviews on the need for a more effective performance management system. Communication and teamworking also figured high on their list of priorities. In relation to the former, speak-up sessions with groups of staff (n = 15) have been carried out throughout the organisation each autumn, and the CEO tried to attend all the induction sessions for new starters. Team-building exercises with teams of clinical staff had been central to the training activities during the last year, and that was seen as important. One of the biggest challenges faced by Case 5 is recruitment and retention, especially due to competition from the private sector and agencies.

Work–life balance and appraisal

Case 6 is also a PCT where several directors referred to appraisal and work–life balance as the major HR issues at their organisation. The thrust to ensure that every member of staff should have a performance review and development plan was championed personally by the CEO, and coverage had increased dramatically over the last few years. Work–life balance focused on a number of areas – for example, nine-day fortnights. However, one director felt that although admirable as an objective, this was extremely hard to achieve because the Trust was trying to modernise services while aiming to reduce working hours. Results from the staff survey were good, appraisal and feedback falling in the top 20% for equivalent Trusts (see Figure 7 on page 25) and job satisfaction levels were high – although so too was reported work pressure.

What is interesting from the interviews with the senior management teams at each Trust was how they put a slightly different emphasis and priority on the range of HR practices. Admittedly, certain HR practices regularly reappeared in these accounts – eg employee involvement, teamworking and appraisal – but the emphasis varied between Trusts, as did the way they went about developing these practices.

PERFORMANCE PROFILES

Performance measurement frameworks in the NHS

The system for assessing the performance of NHS organisations changed from 2005 onwards. Prior to that time, a 'star rating' system had been used – organisations were awarded from 0 to 3 stars annually following external assessment of a range of factors (Hyde *et al*, 2006a). There was 'a general view that the star ratings ... did not represent a rounded or balanced scorecard of ... performance' (Mannion *et al*, 2005; p.18).

From 2005 onwards a new system was introduced, described as the Annual Health Check. This system of annual review combines data from a number of sources, and assesses how well the organisation is both meeting a set of core standards and developing for the future (Hyde *et al*, 2006a). For 2005/6 the developmental standards assessment was not, however, used because it was not fully developed. It is claimed (Healthcare Commission website) that

> *It's far more wide-ranging and tougher than the old system of star ratings, which only looked at how the NHS was performing in relation to targets set by the Government ... [It] goes much further. It scores NHS Trusts on many aspects of their performance, including the quality of the services they provide for patients and the public and how well they manage their finances and other resources such as their property and staff. These scores are based on a range of information gathered throughout the year.*

The case study sites were selected to be relatively 'high performers' using the star rating system which gives objective and nationally comparable measures of performance. During the period of research the performance assessment system changed to the Annual Health Check and so for completeness the ratings in this system are also shown (see Table 11 below).

In terms of relative positions it is important to understand how these ratings compare with all Trusts in England. This comparison is shown in percentage terms in Figure 5 for star ratings and in Figure 6 for the Annual Health Check ratings, both on page 24.

Table 11 ❖ Case study organisations' performance history

Trust	2002/3	Star ratings 2003/4	2004/5	Annual Health Check 2005/6 Quality of services	Use of resources
Case 1 (Acute)	★ ★ ★	★ ★ ★	★ ★ ★	Good	Fair
Case 2 (Acute)	★	★ ★ ★	★ ★ ★	Good	Fair
Case 3 (Mental Health)	★	★ ★ ★	★ ★ ★	Good	Fair
Case 4 (Mental Health)	★ ★ ★	★ ★ ★	★ ★ ★	Good	Excellent
Case 5 (PCT)	★ ★	★ ★	★ ★	Good	Fair
Case 6 (PCT)	★	★ ★	★ ★	Fair	Fair

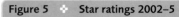

Figure 5 ❖ Star ratings 2002–5

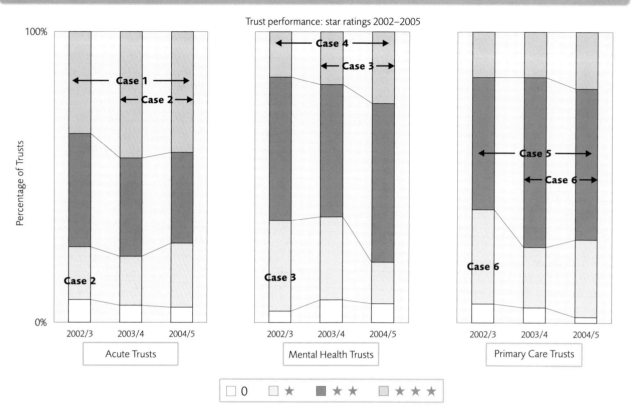

Figure 6 ❖ Annual Health Check performance ratings 2005–6

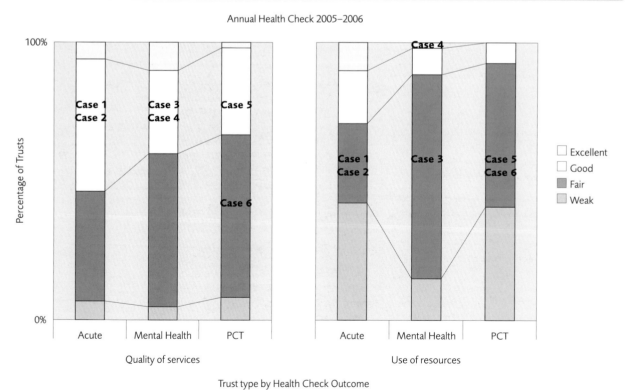

So although all our case sites were considered to be 'high performers' in terms of the old rating (apart from the PCTs) the different methods of assessment under the Annual Health Check process have shown them not to be among the highest performers nationally. In both types of assessment there is a 'balanced scorecard' – ie it is more than simply financial or productivity measures that are used.

The move to the new hospital at Case 2 impacted on their ability to meet two core standards which were both related to HRM.

In relation to core standard C11b, 'Healthcare organisations ensure that staff concerned with all aspects of the provision of healthcare participate in mandatory training programmes', it was noted by the Healthcare Commission that

> *There has been a decrease in the numbers of staff undertaking mandatory training demonstrated in the staff survey possibly due to problems in releasing staff during the relocation of staff into the new hospitals and new clinical teams.*

And in relation to core standard C08b, 'Healthcare organisations support their staff through organisational and personal development programmes which recognise the contribution and value of staff, and address, where appropriate, under-representation of minority groups', it was noted that

> *There has been a decrease in the uptake of appraisals demonstrated in the staff survey possibly due to new clinical teams and accountabilities occurring as a result of the moves to the new hospital, due to changes in management arrangements in the operations directorate and changes in the appraisal process to incorporate KSF.*

In both events the Trust put in place plans to address these issues which will be monitored by the Healthcare Commission.

The NHS staff survey

However, there are other sources of information about performance which are relevant to this research. Figure 7, below, shows various HR indicators taken from the annual NHS staff survey carried out on behalf of the Healthcare Commission. The results of this also feed in to the Annual Health Check assessment of performance. This shows that case study organisations 1, 3, 4 and 6 were consistently high performers. Case 5's scores were largely average but it had made some significant improvements on the previous year. In comparison, Case 2's scores indicated a below-average performance on most HR indicators. However, it had also made some significant improvements since the previous year.

Figure 7 ✚ **Selected staff survey indicators 2006**

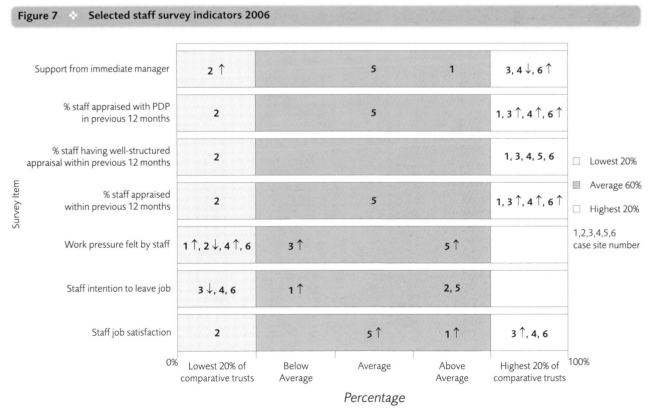

NB An upward arrow shows an increase from th previous year

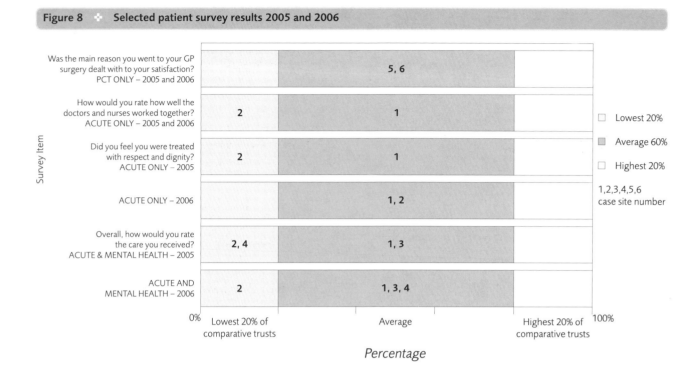

Figure 8 ❖ **Selected patient survey results 2005 and 2006**

The NHS annual patient survey

The Healthcare Commission carries out several patient surveys each year, focused on different aspects of healthcare. A selection of results for the case study organisations is shown in Figure 8. This shows patient satisfaction scores to be in the bottom 20% for Case 2 (Acute Trust in-patient survey) and community mental health scores in the bottom 20% for Case 4 in 2006. None of our case sites was in the top 20% for any measure of patient satisfaction.

However, it is questionable whether the results of such surveys really do reflect the overall standard of patient care. Chapter 9 discusses in more detail the various elements that comprise patient care, and shows that patient satisfaction with their interaction with staff is only one element of patient care and although important, can only ever be one element of overall performance.

CONCLUSION

This chapter has described the six case study organisations in which this research was carried out. They are all NHS organisations, selected specifically to be relatively high-performing. However, they are different in terms of how they interpret national guidance and priorities both in overall organisational strategy and in HRM systems. Subsequent chapters explore these differences in more detail.

LEARNING POINTS

For the organisation as a whole

- The process of developing and then monitoring strategy at both organisational and HRM level is something that involved staff at most case study organisations, although detailed mechanisms varied.

  Involvement in developing and monitoring strategy can be enabled both through formal structures – eg partnership with staff-side representatives – and through informal engagement with individuals.

- Case 6 illustrated effective communication, the organisational strategy, and the associated annual objectives, being widely publicised. The HRM strategy then linked clearly to these objectives.

  The power of effective and simple communication to engage staff in organisational and HRM strategy and implementation needs to be recognised and exploited.

- Case 4 demonstrated that alignment between various elements of organisational strategy was possible, having taken the opportunity of Foundation status to review its strategies, so that every activity now supports the business.

  It is possible to align all elements of strategy with the overall direction of the organisation – including the HRM strategy – and organisations should ensure that there is opportunity to do this.

For the HRM system and the HR function

- The two case study organisations that had obtained Foundation status were clear about the opportunities it gave them for closer involvement with both the community and their staff.

  HRM has a key role in ensuring that such opportunities are maximised and translated into meaningful opportunities for staff involvement.

- Most of the case study organisations retained elements of national guidance as part of their local HRM strategy but had tailored them to their own situations.

  It is important that any national guidance on HRM is interpreted and applied locally, in line with the intention of the NHS as a whole and its direction of travel.

- The implementation and emphasis on various HR practices varied between case study organisations

  It is important to recognise that one size will not fit all, and that local adaptation of HR practices and different emphases, depending on the organisational strategy, will be required.

- All the case study organisations linked the HR function in some way to the operational units of the organisation.

  Structural links to operating units must be established, but also supported in practice by HR staff attending meetings and establishing communication channels that will enable HRM to be put into practice more effectively.

HRM AND PERFORMANCE – WORKING WITH OTHER ORGANISATIONS

✤ **The form and nature of cross-organisational contracting varied across organisations and was affected by the types of arrangements and structures put in place to manage relationships.**

✤ **Ambiguity and complexity in cross-organisational working was increased by fragmented relationships and differences in pay, terms and conditions.**

✤ **Enablers included continuity of service provision from a patient perspective supported by close relationships between organisations.**

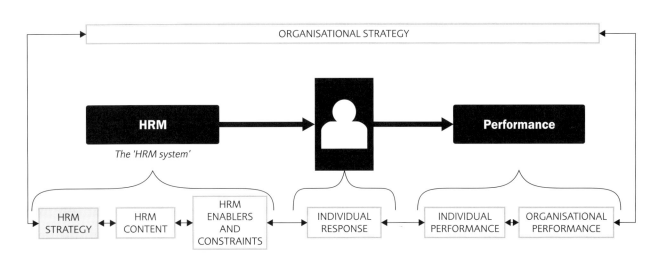

WHAT DOES THIS CHAPTER COVER?

The previous chapter illustrated the wide variety of HR provision in terms of HRM strategy and structure in the case study organisations. This chapter examines the implications for the strategic HRM decision of whether to contract out services, to work in partnership or to maintain in-house provision. It also considers how these decisions operate in practice. Contracting, outsourcing and partnership arrangements at three of the case study organisations are considered and findings are presented in five broad sections:

✤ the form and nature of cross-organisational contracting

✤ ambiguity and complexity in cross-organisational working

✤ positive effects

✤ negative effects

✤ the enablers of positive effects.

WHAT IS THE CONTEXT?

Over the last decade, NHS Trusts have made increasing use of contracted-out services to, or partnerships with, other organisations. Research has typically examined the *consequences* of these decisions for HRM, and it has often concluded that people working for contractors or partners enjoy worse terms and conditions of employment than those who are employed by NHS Trusts (Morgan *et al*, 2000; Domberger *et al*, 2002). Although this may be accurate, particularly if the decision to outsource was taken in order to reduce costs, it is not inevitable because employers make strategic choices about how they want to structure future employment in order to deliver effective patient care. Accordingly, decisions about externalising employment may be driven by other forces, such as a desire to maintain levels of patient care, which can lead to contracted staff being provided with similar terms and conditions, levels of training and employee voice as those working for the NHS (CBI, 2006). Moreover, because decisions about contracting reflect *strategic choices* made by employers, these also impact on staff that are employed by the NHS and who work alongside people employed by other organisations across networks (Marchington *et al*, 2005).

It will be apparent from the preceding paragraph that we would not expect to find one single model of how HRM operates across organisational boundaries, even in an environment where there is a considerable standardisation and co-ordination. Employers vary in their choices about how much to externalise employment in order to meet their goals, some favouring the retention of most services in-house whereas others are prepared to enter into commercial arrangements (eg a PFI) to provide services. Even when decisions are made to engage in contracting, employers vary in how they interact with external providers. Some prefer to operate at arms' length from the organisations to which they have contracted out services and rely on key performance indicators as a monitoring device, whereas others decide it is better to work closely with partners and, wherever possible, maintain similar HR policies and practices across the network.

It is important therefore to locate any analysis of HRM across organisational boundaries within the context of the role that the HR function is allowed or encouraged to play, and the extent to which good employment is embedded within public service provision (CBI, 2006). In addition, in response to pleas for research to be more theoretically informed, particularly in the area of contracting (Ferlie and McGivern, 2003), we move away from concept of the single employer and attempt to analyse relations through the lens of the multi-employer network.

> ### Contracting, outsourcing and partnership can look very different
>
> Multi-employer organisations take a variety of forms, ranging from the relatively simple outsourced arrangement which is at arms' length through to the more complex partnership in which several organisations aim to integrate large amounts of their operational and HR practices through a relational contract.

WHY IS THIS IMPORTANT?

Performance depends on the skills and knowledge of individuals. Providing clinical services requires service management, ancillary and support services. Any change

in employment arrangements must ensure that performance is maintained.

WHERE DID THE DATA COME FROM?

In order to examine these issues, 30 interviews were analysed from three of the cases (1,4,6), and wherever possible documentary material relating to commercial contracts and HR strategies was used. In addition to using a specific interview schedule (see Appendix 1) for staff from the contractors and boundary-spanning agents, valuable data was also obtained from the Chief Executives/Chairs at three of the cases. This provided a wider organisational context and rationale for the Trust's approach to contracting and partnership, as well as insights into the overall style of management adopted at the case study organisation. Although the HR practices adopted by the Trust for its own employees did not necessarily carry over into the way in which non-employees were treated, information about this did provide a useful benchmark against which to assess any differences in managerial behaviour.

Interestingly, soon after the empirical work for this project had been completed, the 'retention of employment model' was launched for those organisations involved in PFIs. Although this clearly adds a further twist to issues of collaboration across organisational boundaries, none of the cases covered in this section was a PFI.

WHAT WERE THE FINDINGS?

The form and nature of cross-organisational contracting

Although there was evidence of cross-organisational contracting in all six case studies, three were examined in detail, one from each of Acute, Mental Health and PCT. These illustrated a range of experiences. Because they related to different organisational forms and types of individuals and jobs covered by the contract, it allowed for some preliminary comparison of how and why HRM developed in the way it did. The broad details are shown in Table 12 on page 32.

The contracts varied across a number of features. First, they differed in terms of which services and groups of individuals were covered by them. In Case 1 this was restricted to a small number of support staff due to worries that having greater numbers of non-employees would undermine team spirit:

> *Security staff is the only bit that is contracted out – the rest of our staff are in-house. For example, we have our own in-house domestics, porters. I think having those key members of staff as part of your*

*staff, they feel part of a team ... I am not saying the
contracted-out staff wouldn't have a primary interest.
Of course they do, but if they do feel it is their
hospital, it is their services, their relatives could be
using the service, then they take a great pride in that.*

(Director)

At Case 1, there were only about 30 contracted-out staff, and
the contracts on which they were employed to provide
security services had changed hands routinely. Not
surprisingly, staff in these positions had largely negative
feelings towards their current employer whom they saw as
transient and not particularly committed to their interests. The
regular turnover of firms responsible for security work was
reflected in the commercial contract between the
organisations and the low-trust relations that seemed to
pervade the whole contracting relationship. On the other hand
there were a small number of volunteers who had more
positive relations and could point to improved patient outcomes.

By contrast, in Case 4 an entirely different stance was taken by
the senior management team, who had worked hard to form
close relations with the contractors and partner organisations.
Although this might be expected when contracts are between
different employers in the public sector, and for contracts
involving professional staff, evidence of positive high-trust
relations was also apparent in relations between the NHS Trust
and private sector providers of services such as cleaning and
catering. In this case, the Trust was one of the highest performers
in mental health and it was keen to be seen as an employer of
choice. For example, the CEO saw staff employed by the Trust
in regular, informal meetings, and accessibility to staff was
regarded as a priority, although he did not specifically meet
with contracted staff in the same way. New contracts had to
focus on factors other than price and the organisation required,
before it became obligatory in such organisations, that NHS
pay rates were mandatory for staff. During contract negotiations,

*We look for how flexible they are in work–life
balance, Investors in People – all the sorts of things
we would expect to offer our employees. It's not easy,
because they are not our employees and a lot of these
people work part-time.*

(Manager)

Contracts were for longer periods of time (five years) and that
with the major cleaning firm (covering about 135 staff: 50
FTEs) had just been renewed, and indeed extended to other
sites. Trust between the two organisations seemed high, as
exemplified by the way in which each spoke about the other.
Frequent meetings took place, both formally and informally,
between the boundary-spanning agents in the two organisations.
For example, the manager for the cleaning contract said:

*I think the key thing is the relationship we've got with
each other. I would think a good 50% of my time is
actually spent going out seeing how things are and
generally chatting to the NHS staff.*

(Director, cleaning contractor)

Similar principles were applied in partnerships (enabled
through Section 31 partnership arrangements) with a number
of local authorities, which covered approximately 130 social
workers and community practice nurses. This was a more
recent contract, and it was complicated by the fact it involved
several different local authorities, but nevertheless all the
employers operated according to a common principle of 'social
inclusion'. Collaboration was also facilitated because the
Director of Partnerships at the Trust had worked previously as
a senior manager at one of the local authorities.

> ## What helps to create better relationships between employers across the network?
>
> ❖ Institutional support through policy initiatives
>
> ❖ Long-term and repeat contracts
>
> ❖ A joint commitment to embedding good employment practice
>
> ❖ High levels of trust between senior managers in partner organisations
>
> ❖ Regular meetings between managers at the partners to share ideas and deal with problems.

In some ways, Case 6 had the most developed form of cross-
organisational working, referred to by one director as it 'feeling
like one organisation' rather than two or more. Collaboration was
provided by an agreement across the local authority and health
services, with staff appointed to work across the partnership –
albeit on employment contracts with different employers. The
relationship at this case study site had been formalised into an
eight-year plan, with high levels of cross-organisational working,
and a clear set of goals to be achieved over each year of the
'journey' towards integrated service provision. The PCT also had
close working relationships with other parts of the NHS – in
acute services or mental health, for example.

*We formed the health and well-being partnership
board which is jointly chaired by the leader of the
Council and the Chair of the PCT. On the board are*

Table 12 ❖ Case study organisations and contracts examined			
	Case site 1	Case site 4	Case site 6
Type of contract examined at case	Commercial contract	Two specific types of contract: (a) commercial (b) Section 31 partnership arrangement (Health Act 1999)	Section 31 partnership arrangement across health and social services
Number of staff involved in contracts	Approx 30 security staff, including car parking	(a) 135 cleaners (b) 130 social workers, community practice nurses	Social workers, community practice nurses, physiotherapists. GPs contracted to provide services for the PCT
Reasons for contracting out/ setting up partnership	Cost reductions.	(a) Cost, quality and reliability (b) Integration of seamless service	Goal to 'improve the quality of lives of local people'. Partnership includes housing and environment
Length of contract	Repeat and new contracts over 10 years, all short-term	(a) Five years. Contractor just won more contracts across Trust (b) Started three years ago and about to be renewed	Eight-year plan in operation. Joint appointments being made to permanent contracts
Degree of trust demonstrated by each party	Poor. Security staff employed at Trust worked for several agencies. Requirement of contract to keep existing staff	(a) High. Steering group keen on quality. Regular, positive contact between managers. Based at same site (b) High. Contact for five years before partnership. Shared vision of social inclusion	High. Shared vision and long-term plan to align goals to meet targets built into strategy
Organisational forms for each contract	Trust holds power in relationship. Security staff feel attachment towards Trust. Minimal contact/engagement with agency	(a) Penalty clauses in contract but not invoked yet. Both large organisations so relative power balance (b) Director of Parnerships at Trust worked at one of local authorities. Many partners across public and voluntary sectors	Have not merged PCT and social services to form a Care Trust, so the organisations retain their forms. Joint CEO for PCT and Social Services. Moving to joint appointments wherever possible
Nature of HR requirements for each contract	Terms negotiated by union and agency. Not on NHS pay rates	(a) Contractor pays NHS rates. HR Helped to draw up contract: IiP, training systems, appraisal, etc. Contractor keen to be seen as quality supplier (b) Integrated working. Some common policies (eg appraisal) but others different (eg pay, grievance)	Moving to shared HR services across partner organisations. PCT HR director now covers social services through a joint contract. Still some variations in terms and conditions

three non-executive directors from the PCT, three elected members in addition to the joint chairs, and the local authority Chief Executive and the PCT Chief Executive act as professional advisers to that board.

(Director)

Why do contract and partnership relationships differ?

Contracting and partnership relations take quite different forms in the three cases examined here. Much of the difference, in terms of strategic intent, can be explained by the nature of the institutions and structures put in place to manage the relationship, and also by the types of individuals and services involved. However, although clearly shaping the way relationships developed, formal processes do not explain all the differences. For example, differences between Cases 1 and 4 involving individuals in similar types of role are shaped by the quality of on-going relations between partners, and the levels of trust between them, as well as the influence that seeking to be a good employer can have over subsequent HR outcomes.

Ambiguity and complexity in cross-organisational working

Inevitably, ambiguities and complexities arise in any situation where staff work across organisational boundaries. Not surprisingly, these were most pronounced in the looser and more fragmented relationships, where staff had experienced a number of different employers over the last few years as contracts changed hands. This was summed up by one of the security staff:

When I started off, it was somebody called A. They lost the contract and somebody called B got it. They were here a long time, Company B. And they lost it and C got the contract from them.

(Manager, private security firm)

Interestingly, this impacted more negatively on the private companies than it did on the NHS Trust, and indeed, each of the individuals we interviewed referred to the Trust in glowing terms. This was substantiated by the manager overseeing the contract, who was employed by the Trust:

Their loyalty is to me and the Trust. It's irrespective of who pays their salary. They are very much part and parcel of the Trust. They support what we do.

(Manager)

In Case 4, similar tensions arose because cleaners saw better career opportunities by being directly employed by the Trust, something that was facilitated as they got to know patients and staff by remaining on the same wards. It also acted as a sort of pre-employment filtering device for the NHS. Similar ambiguities, again relating to loyalty, arose with professional staff, and especially with social workers employed by local authorities but permanently based at one of the Health Service establishments. One of the social workers summed it up:

It's difficult. You are employed by the one, so you have loyalty to them. But you're managed by the other, so you inevitably have a bit of loyalty to them as well. In a way, you start seeing yourself as being employed by the Trust because you only really have contact with them.

(Social worker)

Issues of loyalty and commitment were not the only area where ambiguities arose, and even in Case 6 inevitable questions surfaced about differences in pay and terms and conditions between staff employed by separate organisations. Disparities caused some tensions:

Where you've got people working in integrated teams, there is some disparity on occasions between salary levels. And although we've sort of ridden that, I think there there's an underlying tension that could bubble away.

(Manager)

Within integrated teams, because staff remained on slightly different terms and conditions, one individual suggested that there was an element of pick-and-mix among staff who opted for those arrangements that made them better off irrespective of who was their employer. Others agreed that having more than one set of HR practices to work with led to ambiguities, and prevented them from having a clear grasp of precisely what was relevant to which member of staff.

Enablers

In the light of the limited extent of contracting at Case 1, it is not surprising to find little evidence of positive links between the work of the security staff and patient care. In a way, whatever the situation, it is difficult for groups such as these to see an explicit connection between what they do and patient care, a situation made more problematic because of grievances about the level at which parking fees had been set.

In Case 4, the relatively strong relationship between the Trust and the contractor also seemed to result in positive effects rather more often than negative ones. The stance of the Trust in requiring high levels of investment and professionalism from the contractor, and then monitoring this, was seen as having a positive impact on patient care.

I suppose only through insisting that these companies operate appropriate training set-ups and they undertake their appraisals. We check those at regular intervals. I will go down there and say, 'That cleaner you took on four weeks ago – can I have look at their induction form, please?' So I guess it's only by appraisal and training that the patient can benefit.

(Manager)

Several individuals in Cases 4 and 6 reported that positive effects came about because patients were no longer confused at the sight of professionals who were quite obviously employed by different organisations. In Case 4, for example, it was argued that patients in the mental health units could not differentiate between social workers and community practice nurses when they came onto the premises, and that services could be provided by either professional. This led to benefits for patients, and a more seamless service to patients, rather than fixating on job demarcations between staff, although there are clear limits to what different professionals can do:

> *Certainly, social workers don't give medication and nurses don't carry out approved social worker assessments. But it could be a nurse or it could be a social worker as your care coordinator.*

(Director)

Similar sentiments were evident at Case 6, both in terms of how HR issues were handled and for patient care. Regarding the former, appraisals were done by the relevant service manager – who might be from a social work or a nursing background – making use of the Trust's procedures. Similarly, restructuring led to improvements in terms and conditions for occupational therapists, which meant that the Trust could now attract sufficient well-qualified staff rather than having to rely on agency staff as it had in the past. Moreover, good HRM practice could be learned from either organisation. Of course it was recognised that differences of opinion and lack of trust between individuals employed by different organisations might not disappear altogether, but closer working could offer routes to deal with conflicts:

> *When you sit round the table there'll clearly be differences of opinion or views. But it's very clear what the shared objective is … And the mere fact that you're sitting on the same floor as health means that I don't have to set up a meeting. We've got that day-to-day dialogue which underpins the processes.*

(Manager)

Overall, therefore, there is evidence from each case that cross-organisational working can help to minimise differences in employer goals so as to satisfy patient needs. This seems to work better when there are close and lasting relations between organisations, and where both partners are prepared to trust the other. Although this might be easier to achieve in contracts between NHS Trusts and local authorities, it is also possible (as seen at Case 4) between public and private sector employers provided the frameworks and goodwill are in place. However, although there were positive examples in each case, there were also a similar number of negative effects.

Constraints

Frustrations about issues such as low pay, lack of voice, or unclear and non-existent appraisal and career development opportunities were expressed at all sites by some staff, although it was not always possible to identify a clear and direct link between individual attitudes and impacts on patient

care. Communications breakdowns appeared to be a problem for a number of contracted-out or partnership staff, in terms of lack of information about changes to systems. For example, local authority staff working at an NHS site did not get access to their own employer's intranet and only found out about changes when they submitted a claim on an outdated form or they heard about a training session after it had taken place. Although justifying this from a patient perspective, one of them summed up the problem for staff quite graphically:

> *From a service-user point of view it works because they have the social workers working in the Trusts where they come for service. So they get holistic care. But you feel isolated from your employer, the local authority, but you also don't fit 100 per cent. It's like being an immigrant in another country, basically. You no longer belong where you came from but you also don't fit in exactly where you've been sent.*

(Social worker)

In the short term this may not present an immediate problem in respect of patient care, but there are limits to how long positive impacts can be maintained if staff frustrations with HR practices continue. Being part of two large organisations operating at Case 6, and on the margins of both, led to concerns about problems with communication and lack of voice, especially in a climate where major changes were taking place regularly.

Enablers and constraints

Although negative effects were found, brought about or exacerbated by cross-organisational working, there were many positive outcomes to report. How much is this due to the fact that people working for non-NHS organisations, especially those that have been transferred, still show a strong commitment to patient care?

Most seriously, despite all the efforts that were taking place at Case 6 to integrate services, the impact on HRM was not always positive – for example, in relation to getting clearance for new or replacement posts:

> *Because it was a Social Services post, it meant that in creating the job description and person specification it's got to be agreed with the union and also senior officers. Then it has to be finally agreed by the portfolio-holder for health and social care before the post is established, and then advertised. And I find the actual process very long-winded and very frustrating.*

(Manager)

CONCLUSIONS

There is little doubt that the provision of services by staff working for a number of different employers at the same site has the potential to weaken service delivery to patients, especially where trust and collaboration between partners is low. However, it is also clear that positive effects are achievable, and that even if people working for contractors or partners do not feel particularly enamoured by their employer's HR practices, they tend to be professional enough to minimise the impact on patient care.

A number of factors seem to increase the likelihood of positive effects:

❖ Higher levels of institutional support (eg section 31) which create a positive framework of governance and accountability within which different employers can work, and which help to shape HRM

❖ Evidence that senior managers at organisations across the network are prepared to work positively with each other in a relational climate of trust rather than arms' length and transactional relationships between organisations.

❖ Requirements that certain underlying principles of 'good' HRM govern the practices that contractors are expected to offer staff, in terms of pay, communications and training, among others

❖ Elements in commercial contracts that help to shape and sustain more positive effects, such as longer and repeat contracts, agreed procedures for monitoring HR in practice, seeking reliability and high quality, rather than going for the cheapest provider

❖ Close links between managers working for different employers, in part provided by structural arrangements (such as regular formal meetings) but also by willingness by both organisations to support high-trust relations between boundary-spanning agents.

WHAT ARE THE LINKS WITH THE REST OF THE RESEARCH?

❖ Organisational strategy will affect the HRM strategy and the extent to which contracting out services is a part of this.

❖ The impact of working with other organisations can be seen in both HR content (where HRM systems are not aligned between the various organisations) and in terms of performance.

HRM AND PERFORMANCE – WORKING WITH OTHER ORGANISATIONS

LEARNING POINTS

❖ Path dependency can be seen where good long-term relations between partners enable the development of shared understanding of performance and patient care.

❖ A cumulative effect in terms of a continued focus on patient care is seen in staff who previously worked for the NHS but now work for partner organisations.

❖ Senior managers at organisations across the network need to work positively with each other in a relational climate of trust rather than arms' length and transactional relationships between organisations.

❖ NHS organisations must recognise the value in forging relationships with private sector employers committed to similar principles and ways of working – ie whose approach is aligned with their own – and detail this in terms of policy, practice and communication mechanisms.

❖ Certain underlying principles of 'good' HRM should govern the practices that contractors are expected to offer staff, in terms of pay, communications and training, among others.

For the organisation as a whole

Ensure that people working for partners and contractors are fully aware of NHS goals regarding patient care.

Ensure that the positive attitudes that most people working for partners and contractors have towards providing patient care are maintained.

Set up and facilitate a series of working teams at different levels, comprising managers from the NHS and partner/contractor organisations in order to develop positive working relationships.

For the HRM system and the HR function

Guarantee that contracts with external providers contain clauses stipulating a similar philosophy of 'good' HRM practice among partners and contractors, with detail of policy, practice and communication on these issues.

Implement processes and procedures for embedding and monitoring 'good' HRM practice at regular intervals after contracts have been signed off. This may involve joint monitoring by both parties.

HR CONTENT – UNDERSTANDING, PRACTICES AND PERCEPTIONS

5

❖ **HRM was perceived most commonly as the HR function, especially at lower levels of the organisation.**

❖ **HR practices were grouped into three bundles relating to: professional development, employee contribution and the employee 'deal'.**

❖ **HR practices were perceived to act as enablers or constraints to performance depending on whether or not they benefited the individual and/or organisation.**

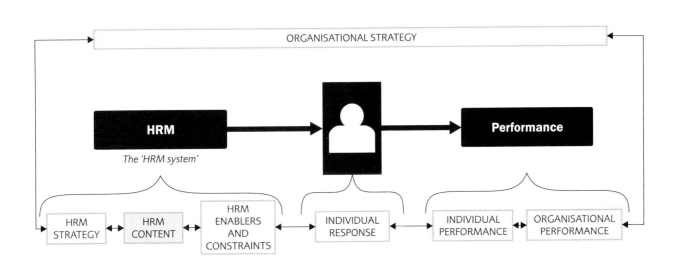

WHAT DOES THIS CHAPTER COVER?

This chapter describes:

❖ an understanding of how HRM was perceived within the organisation (ie from the perspective of individuals)

❖ how individuals made sense of HR practices in terms of how they think they are bundled together

❖ the reasons used by individuals to explain these beliefs

❖ how single HR practices were perceived in terms of whether they were positive gains for the individual, the organisation, both, or neither.

> *Key Concept*: **MENTAL MODELS**
>
> 'Mental models' are frameworks developed by individuals to describe, explain, and predict behavior (Norman, 1983; Rouse and Morris, 1986). A mental model (of, for example, a computer, a job, or a process such as strategy development) reflects the individual's perception of reality (Brunswik, 1956).

WHAT IS THE CONTEXT?

In the first stage of this project, a systematic literature review was conducted on research undertaken on HRM and performance (see Hyde *et al*, 2006a). From this, it was clear that there is considerable variation about which HR practices might be included in a bundle, in how a specific HR practice might be evaluated, and in the desired performance outcomes that might therefore result from the practice.

There remains considerable debate surrounding the links between HR practices and individual performance outputs and between particular bundles of HR practices aimed at improving performance outcomes. Additionally, arguments have been made for better understanding of individual perceptions of HR practices in order to understand how these might affect the quality of implementation (Harris *et al*, 2007). Although academics have strong theoretical views on which HR practices are important and how they might be combined together (see, for example, Boxall and Purcell, 2003; Boselie *et al*, 2005), it is rare for individuals to be asked how HR practices are experienced in their working lives. We used the list of 11 HR practices which we had generated as being relevant to the NHS (see the section describing HR content in Chapter 2).

WHY IS THIS IMPORTANT?

Individuals have implicit mental models of how HRM impacts on patient care that are based upon experience and their insights into practice and help explain how HRM is perceived and how it can contribute to improved performance. A way of understanding these models is to get individuals to articulate how specific practices are combined, and then to explain the reasons why the practices are linked – ie the outcomes that result from the combination of practices. It is important to understand this for several reasons:

❖ Individuals might not even know or understand wider organisational goals, so that variance in how practices are perceived might occur due to poor communications from senior managers or the HR function or by line managers.

❖ HR practices may be perceived differently by individuals at various levels in the hierarchy. The HR practices that senior managers assume are put in place might be perceived rather differently by those who are in direct contact with patients or are responsible for the line management of staff.

❖ Individuals might feel that the direction of the organisation is not appropriate for generating improvements in performance, but prefer to operate in a way that they feel is more beneficial to patient care. By revealing how and why individuals believe that HR practices relate to each other, it should be easier for the HR function to understand what is important for HR strategies to produce their desired effect within the NHS.

WHERE DID THE DATA COME FROM?

The first part of this chapter contains information provided in response to the question: 'What is HRM?' (see Appendix 1).

The remainder of the chapter provides an analysis based on a card-sorting exercise through which individuals were asked to group 11 practices and to offer explanations for these groupings. At the end of the interview participants were given a series of cards, each with a specific HR practice written on it, and were asked to illustrate how these practices related to each other and how they helped them do their job.

WHAT WERE OUR FINDINGS?

Perceptions of HRM

Responses to the question 'What is HRM?' were classified in five categories:

❖ the personnel function

❖ the HR function

❖ people management

❖ having an impact on delivering performance

❖ 'don't know': when the individual was unable to say what HRM constituted.

Over half the individuals (55%) equated HRM to the HR function. All pay bands and job classifications referred to HRM as the HR function and the same finding occurred across all six case study sites.

However, within the spread of responses, there were some variations according to pay band and job type. Although nearly two-thirds of individuals on the lowest pay bands (1–4) were likely to refer to HRM as the HR function (64%), only 41% of individuals on the highest pay bands did so (band 8 and directors).

The way in which HRM (both the HR function and the notion of people management) is seen at the highest level of the organisation affects legitimacy and influence more broadly within the organisation, so it is important to understand how HRM is perceived from a board-level perspective. In all case sites, the HR directors were board members, and other board members recognised the importance of HRM:

> *I probably wouldn't say this to the HR Director, but it is absolutely vital. We are a people business in the health service; it is all about the patient–doctor or doctor–nurse interaction. The evidence is that if you get that interface right, you're well on the way to not only making patients better quicker but being a much more efficient organisation as well.*

(Director)

IMPROVING HEALTH THROUGH HUMAN RESOURCE MANAGEMENT

Mental models and groups of HR practices

Although there was some variability in groupings, there were some very clear patterns (60 individuals produced 91 groupings), two other staff could not relate the practices, and three staff said they all link together. The most common groupings of HR practice were:

❖ appraisal, training and career development (or a combination of any two of these) – 31 responses

❖ communication, teamworking and employee involvement (or a combination of any two of these) – 26 responses

❖ recruitment, pay, non-monetary rewards, work–life balance and job security (or a combination of two or more of these) – 20 responses.

Less frequently, links were made between:

❖ teamwork and training – 3 responses

❖ appraisal and communication – 3 responses.

1   Professional development

This first set of connections – appraisal, training and career development – clearly signals that individuals see themselves as part of a professional and vocational organisation in which development of skills is important. The key expressions that individuals used to explain the linkage of these HR practices revolve around points such as doing the job better, filling gaps in knowledge, training requirements, service development and (linked to these objectives) personal career development. Clearly, the contribution that these individuals made to improved patient care is perceived to be dependent upon the quality of skills and knowledge that individuals possess, and thus relates to appropriate appraisal, training and career development. Although individuals referred to a series of organisational outcomes when grouping these HR practices, there is also an element of self-interest. Up-to-date and relevant professional knowledge serves individual career needs as well.

Three quotes sum up well the links between these HR practices and show how they combine together, at both an organisational and an individual level. They demonstrate the critical role that professional development plays in the NHS context. The first quote, from a senior manager, displays a relatively integrated approach, viewing the process as providing mutual gains.

I have got career development, appraisal and training all together, and again I think for a lot of our workforce they would flag up that these are incredibly important and something that this organisation does very, very well. So we know what people's needs are through the joint process of appraisal. We know what their wants are as well through that opportunity, and then we can look at where that might take them and what training and development they need alongside that.

(Director, HR)

The other quotes, from more junior staff, assess the links more in terms of individual development and how that might contribute to improvements in patient care. This is interesting because it shows how professionals in particular tend to think in terms of how career development will benefit the service.

I suppose training goes with appraisal because by appraising yourself you realise that there are gaps in your knowledge ... and then you can address those. And I suppose career development I would link in, and again that's giving you direction. You can use [your training] within your role and develop your service.

(Physiotherapist, pay band 7)

To give good patient care, you've got to have training, obviously – on-going training as well. And your appraisals come into that because when you have appraisals you're discussing how you're doing your job, how you can improve, etc. Any way that you can improve obviously helps with patient care.

(Health care support worker, pay band 2)

THE NHS ELECTRONIC STAFF RECORD (ESR)

The ESR is described as a key building-block in the modernisation of the NHS, following the NHS Plan (DH, 2000) and is a national technology solution which is gradually being rolled out across England and Wales. It is claimed that one of its key benefits 'is the integration of data and processes, on a national scale. This means that employee data will need to be entered just once, but can then be used as part of any of the processes.' It has been designed to be used by

HR and Payroll functions with traditional accountabilities, but also to support devolved HR, employee and manager self-service.

The ESR comprises a number of modules, three of which are specifically relevant to this group of HR practices:

❖ 'Learning management' – which includes the administration of training courses, and the recording of training undertaken by every employee. Courses can be linked to defined competencies, including national competence frameworks, so that current employee competencies and progress towards those competencies can be updated and monitored. A wide range of reports enables control over all aspects of staff training and development.

❖ 'Talent management' – which monitors the careers of individuals, maintaining the competencies, qualifications and experience of each staff member and manages their development reviews and training. Employee competencies are maintained within defined national and local frameworks.

❖ 'Self-service' – which allows any staff member to access the system through a simple browser-based interface, with the facility to view and update his or her personal information. Staff can also instigate development reviews, assess training possibilities and request to be enrolled on courses. Managers have some additional facilities, such as approving employee requests, maintaining employee status, and locating staff who are suitable for new job opportunities.

Effective implementation of the ESR will reduce the HR function's role in administrative support processes and enable them to concentrate on other areas of HRM. It also enables individual members of staff to become more involved in managing their own careers through the self-service module.

Sources: www.esrsolution.co.uk and www.esrsolution.co.uk/whatesr/vision

2 Employee contribution

The second set of connections – communication, teamworking and employee involvement – reflects an interest on the part of the NHS workforce in getting engaged with key issues in the organisation, largely because they care about the impact of their actions and the way in which decisions might impact on patients.

As with any service context, performance delivery often depends upon how well teams and individuals communicate and share understanding, and it is clear from individuals that communication within teams, between professional communities and up and down the hierarchy is extremely important for the provision of effective patient care. Drawing upon the key words that individuals used to make sense of this set of HR practices, we can see how individuals are keen to be involved in decisions at work in order to contribute their ideas as well as be informed as much as possible about

developments within the Trust. This is based ideally upon a consultative style, high-quality within-team communication, and an awareness that informal governance helps to provide effective management of service relationships.

In short, where decisions can result in life-and-death situations or where the quality of service is highly dependent upon co-ordination between different groups of staff, both within and external to the Trust, individuals expect positive performance outcomes to flow from communication, teamworking and employee involvement.

Q: **What happened?**
A: *We are shutting hospitals and opening hospitals, and shutting wards. We are going through some major changes. I have been involved in doing new rotas because some hospitals need extra porters and some hospitals need fewer porters.*

Q: **How did it make you feel?**
A: *It is satisfying to know that people value my opinion. It makes me feel valued.*

Q: **What was the impact on your performance?**
A: *When you are valued, your performance does go up because you do feel part of the team. When you are not consulted, your performance goes down because you are just left to carry the can and sometimes you will probably think 'Why was I not consulted?'*

Q: **How did it affect patient care?**
A: *I have been able to put my ideas forward about where we can fit extra beds in, and where we can open other wards to meet the demand from patients.*

(Hotel and estates, pay band 5)

A number of quotes sum up the links between these three HR practices within the general area of employee contribution. Two individuals stressed the critical importance of teamworking and communications both within and between teams, and in one case specifically linked this to patient care.

I suppose [communication] links in with the employee involvement, making those decisions and asking for suggestions. The communication would link in with the teamworking because you can't have a team that works without communication.

(Therapist, pay band 7)

We've got a very strong sense of working as a team within our own profession. The health visitors all really work together and are very supportive. How to do the

IMPROVING HEALTH THROUGH HUMAN RESOURCE MANAGEMENT

job? Communication, employee involvement, definitely. They are the main things that help you do your job.

(Nurse, pay band 6)

Two other members of staff, on lower pay bands within their respective Trusts, felt that communication breakdowns had potentially disastrous implications for patient care and service delivery, and that teamworking and consultative styles were critically important for superior levels of performance and high reliability working in a potentially dangerous environment.

Well, I think if you don't work as a team, it can't all come together. I've always thought that. Then you don't meet your targets or the patients don't get the right sort of care, and that's where communication comes in. Communication is the most important thing – along with teamworking.

(Clerical, pay band 2)

Teamwork? Well if they don't actually pull together as a team, then obviously that can have serious consequences for the standard of care. They do have to work together. You have all got to be aware of what each other is doing and communicate within the team.

(Clerical, pay band 2)

IS THIS SUPPORTED BY OTHER RESEARCH?

Although organisational forms have to allow for variation in the activity being carried out, there has to be stability in the thought processes that individuals use to make sense of their roles. If this culture is disrupted, not only may performance improvements not be achieved but also more serious outcomes can arise from the loss of reliability. Research in health services has shown problems in team-work and communication being linked to service errors (Leonard *et al*, 2004).

3   The employee 'deal'

The third set of connections – recruitment, pay, rewards, work–life balance and security – reflect a perception by individuals that there is an overall employee 'deal' that results from working in the NHS. In return for performance that is based on professional development (the first bundle of HR practices) and employee contribution (the second bundle), there are personal expectations about the more visible HR practices concerning the ability to attract and reward individuals through HR practices such as pay, security and work–life balance.

There are several ESR modules which are relevant to this group of practices:

❖ The 'recruitment' module which manages the entire recruitment process – from the identification of the initial vacancy, through the selection of suitable applicants, to an offer being made to the successful candidate. The data that is captured during this process creates and builds the Employee Record, so this information never has to be entered again.

❖ The 'core HR' module which contains all the core employee information used by other components of the system – it covers new joiners, changes, and leavers.

❖ The 'pay' module which holds all the information needed to produce accurate payments to staff – or draws it from other parts of the ESR system.

❖ The 'absence' module which enables organisations to monitor and manage the times when staff are away from work – including sickness, annual leave, special leave and maternity.

The key outcomes that individuals used to link these HR practices concern a fair return for their efforts not just in terms of pay and non-monetary benefits but also in terms of employment security, as well as some recognition that staff need to achieve an appropriate work–life balance. Although security is part of this bundle of HR practices, the fact that recruitment, pay, non-monetary rewards and work–life balance are combined with this suggests that it represents a more transactional aspect of the psychological contract, not a relational one (see Chapter 7). At the same time, there was a general feeling that pay was not a major motivator for working in the NHS.

I suppose recruitment and pay, and maybe job security – you could put them together. If the nurses felt they were being banded properly, it might encourage new people to apply for the jobs...and maybe the old ones not to leave and look for other jobs.

(Nurse manager, pay band 6)

Obviously, pay – that's the reason everybody comes to work, because they have bills to pay. Job security – again, it goes along with this as you have to pay bills, you want to stay in the same place, you don't want to be moved around, you want to feel comfortable in the environment that you're working in, and you want to

Figure 9 ❖ Responses to HR practices

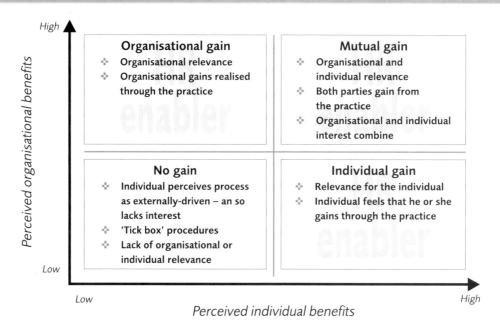

build up your team. You want to feel confident and happy in what you're doing, rather than one week in one job and one in another job. I don't believe you gain confidence from that.

(Nurse, pay band 7)

The important things for me are flexibility in working time. I can go home if there is a personal problem. They provide therapies like head massage, carers' time. The locality of work is ideal.

(Clerical, pay band 3)

The contribution of multiple HR practices to performance

The ability of HR practices to contribute to performance relies to some extent on how sets of practices are delivered and received by individuals. Strong HRM systems develop a climate which improves performance by aligning employee attitudes and behaviours to organisational goals. They are also able to integrate HR practices and processes, the content of HRM, with the process of delivery (Bowen and Ostroff, 2004). The challenge to HRM is to deliver sets of practices which align employee and employer expectations and to renegotiate these expectations to reflect different needs on the part of such a wide range of individuals, and as organisational needs change.

Figure 9, above, illustrates how practices may be perceived to benefit both the organisation and the individual (mutual gains), to benefit the organisation alone (organisational gain), to benefit the individual alone (individual gain) or to benefit neither (no gain).

It can be seen from Figure 9 that an 'ideal' situation could be where both parties to the employment relationship gain from their interactions, with the result that patients are also able to obtain better standards of care within the framework of a more efficient organisation. In certain situations – such as where it is difficult to recruit staff due to tight external labour markets or to factors that reduce the attractiveness of the employer (eg where house prices in the area are very high) – it is likely that both parties will see the value of a mutual gains approach. Conversely, at the opposite extreme, where neither party feels the HR practices in place offer any advantages whatsoever, they tend to be regarded as 'tick box' procedures which are completed as part of a meaningless exercise, and interpreted merely as administrative impositions, originating from outside of local teams. The two other categories in the diagram are where just one party is felt to gain from the HR practice.

Individuals (n = 172) described how or whether each HR practice enabled them to do their job. What is important here is employee responses to these practices and the extent to which individuals were able to use them to support their work. These may be termed the enablers and constraints for HRM at the individual level. These enablers and constraints represent individual interpretations of the practice in individuals' experience. The same practices were interpreted in different ways which constrained or enabled potential effectiveness.

Enablers and constraints of HR practices

Enablers and constraints relate to responses to HR practices perceived to provide gains for both parties, for either the organisation or for the individual, or for no one. In the first of these cases – in which both parties were perceived to gain from the relevant HR practices – there was an expectation (often implicit) that patient care would be improved, or at least would not deteriorate. In the cases where either the individual or the organisation was perceived to gain most, much depended on the specific circumstances of the situation. There are clearly some cases where individuals gain, but these did not necessarily translate into organisational gains as well. For cases that were perceived as primarily an organisational gain, effects also depended on the situation – with the consequence that they might or might not be converted into performance. The final response is where HR practices were perceived as providing gains for no one and merely fulfilling administrative necessity.

Mutual gains

Some of the individuals interpreted HR practices in terms of mutual gains in the sense that they appeared to align employee and organisational expectations, and provide benefits for both parties. This quote shows how appraisal was interpreted as a means of aligning organisational objectives and individual benefits, of integrating different HR practices to achieve mutual gains.

> A whole raft of things comes out of [the] appraisal process, and in many ways apart from training. It does link also therefore to someone's development within the organisation and career development. So I was almost thinking, in a sense, appraisal – we are looking at developing the organisation's needs and goals but in so doing developing the individual and picking up training requirements as we go through.
>
> (Director)

Other quotes illustrate how other bundles of HR practices – especially employee involvement, communication and teamwork – can work together to impact on performance and patient care.

> Teamworking again is vital, as I've explained with the cancer team and the multidisciplinary team administrators, and each of the secretarial teams. I believe in teamworking and I think it helps me to do my job – the Trust to do the job – and overall is a very good thing to have, really ... A bigger team can build on each other's strengths and weaknesses and have a better grasp of things. You can't know everything. There are times when you need your colleague to help you.
>
> (Manager, pay band 8)

> Communications and involvement are critical because they are needed for the job to work. You have got to be able to communicate both with your managers and your staff. If you involve employees in decision-making, then you are likely to get a better result than if they are told what to do. If they have some input, they are more likely to be proactive.
>
> (Manager, pay band 5)

Organisational gain

Some individuals saw little opportunity for mutual gains in the HR practices that were used, viewing them more as a technique for ensuring organisational gain alone. Some of the more critical comments came from lower-grade staff who felt unhappy with decisions about job-banding or regarded management as solely interested in their own gains – for example, in relation to employee involvement or appraisal. The first two quotes below are indicative of this perspective.

> I actually got an increase in pay for doing this job – but they banded me on the lowest band and there is somebody I know that is on the same band as me but gets a hell of a lot more money than me, but doesn't even have the same experience within the NHS ... I could have really have told them to go and shove it, but I didn't want to do that because I wanted to hold this job together.
>
> (Hotel and estates, pay band 3)

> Well, it [employee involvement] is the same thing as appraisal. We are involved, but I don't think it necessarily means anything.
>
> (Support worker, pay band 4)

Others took a more disinterested perspective, seeing HR practices as something that was done to them by the employer, with no obvious benefit for themselves. The two quotes below show how this arose in relation to appraisal and career development.

> I would say career development, training, employee involvement, communication – those are all to do with the organisation, I think, and appraisal as well. They are to do with this local organisation, my employer. They are responsible for this sort of thing.
>
> (Scientist, pay band 8)

> Apart from being given objectives for the year, I never have too much to say at my appraisal because if I've got a problem or I don't like the way something is being done, I can talk about it straight away. I don't have to write it down and wait.
>
> (Hotel and estates, pay band 5)

HR CONTENT – UNDERSTANDING, PRACTICES AND PERCEPTIONS

Individual gain

Here the practice formed part of the relationship between employer and employee. These responses commonly covered career development, rewards, pay, job security and work–life balance. Personal benefits also included opportunities for personal reflection during appraisal and training. The majority of individuals described a complex exchange where pay was offset against other factors such as having the opportunity to do meaningful and rewarding work, having flexible work arrangements, good pension arrangements and job security.

I think to be a nurse you actually don't do it for pay, you do it for love. You've got to really love this job to do it. I used to have my own business and I packed it in to do this. I was a mechanic and there was no reward. OK, you got the money and all that, but it's not a rewarding job just fixing a car. But this is. Everyone needs pay to survive – but that's the last thing you go for.

(Nurse, pay band 6)

You don't come into the NHS for pay – but you have got the security.

(Support worker, pay band 3)

I think my reward is the good terms and conditions of the hospital. The only rewards I can think of. I am on 33 days' holiday plus bank holidays – which you wouldn't get in a normal factory situation. So one of my biggest pluses for working for the NHS is the number of holidays and bank holidays that I get.

(Hotel and estates, pay band 5)

Being appraised, getting some feedback on how you've performed – this lets you know that you're doing your job well. Which I suppose goes hand in hand with career development. Being appraised, you can see where your next step is.

(Administrative, pay band 7)

However, benefits for the individual were changing and reductions in job security meant that individuals were seeking other benefits:

I think the NHS is changing now, isn't it? There are doctors who haven't got a job now. There is a bit of nervousness, especially with branches of medicine being more competitive than others. You are worrying about doing courses and exams earlier and earlier just so you have got more on your CV when you apply for interviews or apply for jobs.

(Doctor)

Pay, work–life balance and job security were interpreted as a transactional element of the employee deal. For example, job security and pay were said to have little relevance by individuals unless they were unhappy with their particular circumstances. Although recruitment is of critical importance to the organisation, it had little relevance for individuals.

No gain

This referred to situations in which there seemed to be no obvious gain from continuing with a particular HR practice. They included individuals failing to see the relevance of a practice but having to participate. For example, a small number of responses described appraisal as an administrative imposition with little individual relevance, serving the goals neither of senior managers nor of policy-makers. Clinical staff tended to describe appraisal as a bureaucratic device, and mandatory training was also perceived as unsatisfactory. Broadly, the interpretation was that the practice had little local relevance.

Appraisal – I don't think that helps me do my job. I think it's about ticking boxes. As long as you tick the boxes, it doesn't matter.

(Nurse, pay band 6)

You get mandatory training – and there is not one person in the place I have ever heard say 'Oh, great! I am on mandatory training.'

(Clerical, pay band 4)

A further set of reasons that HR practices lacked effectiveness included lack of access or unfairness in application of the practice, or the fact that staff were coming towards the end of or not being part of the deal (that is, to some individuals career development and work–life balance were perceived as irrelevant). Lack of access to training and appraisal were most common, whereas unfairness in comparison to others was most common in respect of pay.

As a manager, I should be saying we do all of these things, and we ensure that everybody gets appraisal, everybody gets adequate training, everybody has opportunities to develop their career. But in the real world it doesn't always happen.

(Nurse, pay band 8)

Appraisals? Ad hoc. Doesn't really happen. It depends on what area you are in and how many staff that line manager has to appraise, because a lot of them have too many for one person. Unless you are in a specialised role – eg nursing or junior doctor, where you've got to be seen to do it in order to climb the scale for that post.

(Administrative, pay band 4)

Well, put it this way. When you are doing appraisal, you are asked if you want to do certain things, like education – do you want to do training? Well, we never get the chance. We never get the time.

(Hotel and estates, pay band 2)

There was ambivalence about whether the way things are done are fair, when our own results were considered (see Appendix 1), more senior staff believing more strongly that things are fair:

Statement:	1 strongly agree 2 agree 3 not sure 4 disagree 5 strongly disagree	ANOVA (p<.05, two-tailed)
I think the way things are done is fair	2.55 [not sure]	❖ Directors agree more strongly than pay band 2 and pay band 6 staff

There was a core group of staff across all job types, who suggested that some practices were not part of their deal. For example, opportunities for career development were not relevant to them either because of reaching the end of a career path, being at the top of a pay band, being a director, or lack of interest in progressing. One reason for not wanting to progress a career was in order to maintain work–life balance.

It can be seen therefore that implementation of HR practices can be constrained by individual perceptions, particularly where practices are perceived to be externally imposed. However, there were also practical constraints concerning access to practices and fairness in application.

CONCLUSIONS

The card-sort featuring the 11 HR practices showed that individuals tended to group them into three broad bundles/mental models:

❖ professional development through practices such as appraisal, training and career development

❖ employee contribution through practices such as communication, teamworking and employee involvement

❖ the employee 'deal' through practices such as recruitment, pay, non-monetary rewards, work–life balance and job security.

It was also possible to categorise HR practices according to who gained from them:

❖ the employee and the employer (mutual gains)

❖ the employer alone (organisational gain)

❖ the employee alone (individual gain)

❖ neither party.

Whereas the first three of these categories could be seen as potential enablers of HRM, the last was clearly perceived as a constraint.

What are the links to the rest of the research?

❖ Working across organisations – Maintaining effective team-work when team members are employed by different organisations is a key challenge.

❖ Working with line managers – Line managers form an important conduit for the translation of HR practices and as such they need the knowledge and skills to ensure effective translation.

LEARNING POINTS

❖ There appeared to be a clearer understanding of the role of appraisal and personal development plans from more senior staff, which may reflect a clearer view of the links between strategy and objectives at higher levels of the organisation.

❖ The way in which HRM (both the HR function and the notion of people management) is understood varies according to the level of the organisation. Staff at lower levels more commonly referred to HRM as the HR function, those at higher levels more often expressing understanding of HRM as people management.

❖ The employee 'deal' resulting from working in the NHS is seen by individuals to comprise reward in return for performance that is based on professional development and employee contribution, showing path dependency.

❖ Professional development is important for all types of staff and is viewed as an opportunity to learn new skills that can contribute to patient care.

❖ The contribution of individuals through communication, teamworking and employee involvement is shown to be important by individuals' describing how HR practices support them in their work.

❖ There is an inevitable variation in how individual HR practices are interpreted by individuals.

❖ Some HR practices, such as appraisal, were seen to be aligned in terms of providing both individual and organisational gain. Others were seen as not being aligned with either individual or organisational goals.

For the organisation as a whole

Enable staff at all levels to understand the link between the strategy of the organisation and their own role and development through appraisal.

For the HRM system and the HR function

Develop and support a consistent understanding of HRM as 'people management' throughout the organisation so that HRM can achieve its objectives.

Help provide staff with a fair and equitable 'deal' in return for their continuing contribution to patient care – through, among others, competitive pay and rewards, work–life balance and security.

Ensure that staff are provided with opportunities for developing their professional skills – through focused and integrated systems for appraisal, training and career development.

Implement practices and processes that encourage staff to contribute to key organisational goals – through effective communication, teamworking and employee involvement.

Develop an understanding of variations in interpretation and implement practices as flexibly as possible to allow for this.

Help to align individual and organisational goals through the implementation of bundles of HR practices which can be demonstrated to support these goals. This will then provide gain for both individuals and the organisation.

HR CONTENT – THE ROLE OF LINE MANAGERS

❖ **Although board members reported the involvement of managers in developing policies, in practice line manager engagement with policy development was limited.**

❖ **The main issues facing line managers when implementing HR policies were concerned with their role, their workload and the policies themselves.**

❖ **HRM was rarely included in line manager appraisals.**

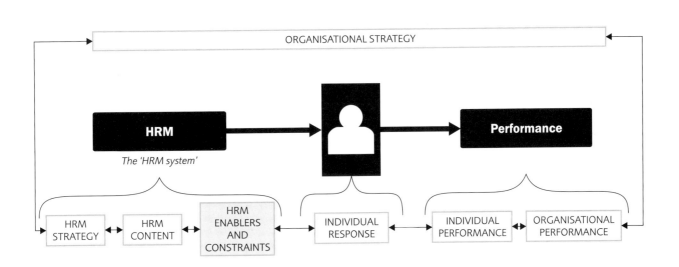

WHAT DOES THIS CHAPTER COVER?

This chapter examines managerial involvement in HRM, and presents findings in the following sections:

❖ The role of the HR function in supporting managerial engagement with HRM

❖ Line manager engagement in developing HR policies

❖ The challenges for line managers.

WHAT IS THE CONTEXT?

A powerful underlying theme in recent HRM–performance research has been the argument that insufficient attention has been paid to the processes that accompany the devolution of particular HR practices and how these are able to embed change at the workplace. This highlights the critical role of immediate line managers in bringing policies to life (see Ulrich, 1997; Whittaker and Marchington, 2003; Marchington and Wilkinson, 2005).

❖ Research by Purcell *et al* (2003) showed that front-line managers have a significant impact on employee attitudes and behaviour, highlighting links between 'front-line leadership' and high levels of employee satisfaction, commitment, motivation and discretion.

❖ Using data from the 2004 WERS survey, Cox *et al* (2007) also show a strong relationship between line managers' approaches to employee involvement and the satisfaction and commitment of individuals, and argue that the informal way in which line managers extend formal employee involvement processes is a key to improved attitudes.

❖ Similar findings in relation to subordinates' feedback-seeking behaviour show an interactive and dynamic relationship between the people management roles of front-line managers and the impact of HR practices (Lam *et al*, 2007).

❖ The idea that line manager behaviour is the critical link between HRM policy and employee performance is supported by work on leader-member exchange theory (see Liden *et al*, 1997, for example) and perceived organisational support (see Eisenberger *et al*, 2002).

Some authors have attempted to examine the balance of responsibilities between managers and HR. For example, Purcell *et al* (2003) highlight how line managers influence a number of HR practices – namely, performance appraisals; training, coaching and guidance, involvement and communication; openness; work–life balance; and recognition. This demonstrates that line managers are perceived to take greater responsibility for certain HR practices – such as dealing with grievances – whereas others, such as pay negotiations, remain the preserve of the HR function.

However, the devolution of HRM to line managers has been problematic, leading line managers to make some deep-seated criticisms of the HR function (Marchington and Wilkinson, 2005). These include:

❖ being out of touch with commercial realities

❖ attempting to maintain too tight a grip on line managers, allowing them far too little discretion

❖ being unresponsive and slow to act

❖ putting forward impractical ideas.

In response, line managers are criticised on a variety of fronts, but in particular for:

❖ lacking skills and knowledge to put HR policies into practice

❖ being dismissive of the HR function and unwilling to learn

❖ lacking consistency in decision-making

❖ having commercial priorities that take precedence over HRM.

As a result, the impression of a negative relationship between line managers and the HR function has evolved.

Because of this, the devolution of responsibility for HRM to line managers can present considerable difficulties. In order to take on HRM responsibility, line managers require skills in HRM and expert advice from a specialist HR function. In addition, devolution suggests higher levels of local discretion for managers and tailored packages and solutions based on two-way dialogue in order to achieve flexibility, choice and fairness (Sparrow and Cooper, 2003).

WHY IS THIS IMPORTANT?

In order to achieve high levels of performance, more is required than simply implementing HR practices – practices have to be embedded throughout the organisation, from the boardroom to the front line. Relationships between the HR function and line managers and managerial engagement with HRM are important mediating factors in this relationship. The image of the HR function throughout the organisation is likely to have an impact on individual perceptions of its role and subsequently on issues of engagement (eg do individuals see HRM as having an important role to play?). It is therefore also important to understand perceptions of how HRM works in the organisation.

WHERE DID THE DATA COME FROM?

Individuals who identified themselves as managers were asked about their level of involvement in HRM, what helped or hindered implementation of HR policies and practices, whether implementation was part of their appraisal, and to what extent the implementation of HR practices was a priority to them. A total of 78 managers were interviewed across the six case sites.

WHAT WERE THE FINDINGS?

The HR function supporting managerial engagement

Despite previous research suggesting a negative relationship between HR and managers, our findings suggest, at these case study organisations, that managers generally experienced supportive relationships with the HR function. When asked what helped them implement HR policies, the majority of individuals across all case sites stated it was the HR team:

We get circulated all the policies and procedures that sit in my office which I share with my colleagues. If you wanted advice on something, yes, you pick up the phone to HR.

(Nurse, pay band 8)

Many other managers echoed this point, indicating that the relationships that had been built with the HR team over time proved valuable in developing confidence to ring up for advice rather than to struggle:

They [our HR department] are very approachable. If you want to speak to them, they will clarify some particular point for you. They are very good at that.

(Manager, pay band 5)

Managers indicated that further support was available from the HRM infrastructure that was in place – specifically, written policies and the intranet – frequently stating that:

They're all available on the Trust intranet. So I just refer to them if I need to. But I can also take advice from the HR team if I need any further information.

(Manager, pay band 5)

Managers were positive about HRM, the majority stating it was a priority to them. Only 6% of individuals specifically stated that HRM was not a priority. Some individuals also differentiated between the HR function and people management, stating that people management or HRM was a priority – especially in their line of work – but this did not mean the HR function alone:

The [HR] department itself isn't a priority, but obviously, HRM is important because we need to make sure that we've got the resources available to continue to deliver the highest quality of care, so we need to make sure staff are in post and there are no vacancies, and that people are managed appropriately and that we look at individual flexibility in roles, and we try to make sure we encourage people to stay within the Trust.

(Nurse manager, pay band 7)

The implementation of AfC was said to have had negative effects on the availability of HR staff to provide support for managers:

If you get stuck, I find that recently the HR department has become quite thin on the ground in our particular Trust and there are very few people to get hold of. In particular with Agenda for Change, a lot of their work has been put to one side so that they can deal with it …

(Lead nurse)

ESR AND THE HR FUNCTION

As the HR function is enabled through the Electronic Staff Record to reduce duplication of effort, with improved reliability of data and improvements to the consistency and quality of workforce reporting, the HR function should be free to concentrate on more strategic aspects of its role (see Figure 10 below). This does not imply that the technology itself will drive change – it is its impact on the work of the HR function that will enable change.

The aim is to transform the HR processes within the NHS from being transactional – mainly concerned with the maintenance of records, form-filling, and responding to queries – to being transformational – concerned with getting value for money, enabling the aspirations of individuals and using information to underpin strategy.

This will clearly affect the support line managers can expect from the HR function, and should enable a more strategic role for HR.

Source: www.esrsolution.co.uk/upload/File/Benefits.pdf

Figure 10   The role of the HR function once the Electronic Staff Record is implemented

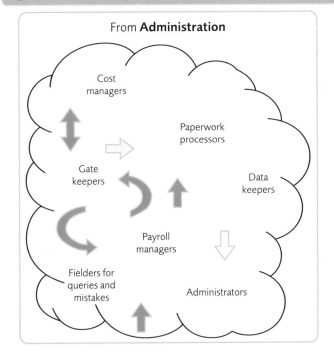

Source: www.esrsolution.co.uk/upload/File/Benefits.pdf

Lack of line manager involvement in the development of HR policies

Board members across all six case sites stressed the importance of line managers in the effective delivery of HRM, insisting that

> when you're developing the policies, you're already creating champions and creating people you know are signed up to them.

(Director, HR)

This affirms the need to develop engagement with HRM.

Board members suggested that when it came to developing new policies 'everyone' was involved. However, closer examination of these statements suggested that 'everyone' does not necessarily equate to those beyond senior management, with no specific reference to the front-line managers who are responsible for implementing HR practices.

> ...HR deliver the policy, but the stakeholder groups contribute... particularly an executive team –we sign it off, for a start! But I tag it to my senior management board, and they feedback for me the impact on themselves ... I would say we are fully involved in developing policies and procedures.

(Director)

This perspective was evident across all six case sites, and the development of local HR policies often occurred at meetings consisting primarily of an executive team. This is not to suggest that line managers were never involved in the development of local policies, but that it occurred infrequently. For example:

> I was involved some years ago when they first implemented the recruitment and selection appointment manual – in about 1997 ...

(Manager, pay band 8)

Why might there be a lack of involvement? This research suggests several possible explanations:

❖ Line managers are not inclined to get involved, and so trying to gain their involvement is difficult. One director explained the lack of managerial involvement as a result of competing priorities and pressures put on them:

> While we try and involve managers in as many different ways and get their views, I am realistic enough to know where the priority is going to lie at the end of the day.

(Manager, HR, pay band 8)

❖ There was a perception that the HR policies themselves are not relevant – something reported by the majority of individuals. They felt that their engagement was more likely to occur when the purpose of the practice was both evident and was felt to have an impact on day-to-day issues.

> Other staff that I work with don't always see why we need this policy. It seems redundant to them because it doesn't actually affect or impact on their work.

(Therapist, pay band 8)

> I think there is a lack of understanding from staff for the reason behind policies ... I suppose that it is partly a managerial shortfall as much as it is an HR one.

(Nurse, pay band 8)

❖ There is also a tendency for national policy to dictate local initiatives. From a line management perspective this resulted in further reductions in discretion about implementation, especially in the face of frequently changing policies. The point was described by directors and more junior staff:

> The national regulation of pay deals in the Health Service has been a major handicap over the past three years. We've lived through the consultant contracts, the Agenda for Change initiative, and the new contracts for local GPs.

(Director)

> If it's been agreed nationally, this is how we're supposed to be doing it. If they are doing something else in the Trust next door, that's up to them – that's their local thing ... and it if blows up, that's their fault!

(Radiographer, pay band 6)

The issues for line managers

The role itself

❖ Increasing line manager involvement in HRM was seen by some to be a part of the job:

> They have devolved quite a lot of work over the last three years to operational managers, clinical managers, and I think we're probably the best people to deal with 90% of the stuff.

(Therapist, pay band 8)

❖ Perspectives typically varied according to the extent to which managers engaged with both the concept of HRM and the HR policies that they needed to implement, some seeing it as very high priority:

HR is the biggest priority in my job because obviously the key part of my job and my responsibilities is managing staff, and that is all about HR management.

(Nurse, pay band 8)

❖ Individuals also reported conflicting priorities and role ambiguity, which is a particular issue in a healthcare context for clinical line managers who have to fulfil both their HRM and clinical responsibilities.

The thing is, you do try to squeeze all these things in. As far as I'm concerned, the patient care comes first, and if I'm late in doing a personal development review, then I'm afraid, well, that's tough. I have to give the priority to the patients.

(Nurse, pay band 8)

❖ Conflicting role priorities often meant that HRM concerns were low on the list of priorities even for non-clinical managers:

If there was a choice to read HR policies or do the thing that you are going to get kicked up the backside from the Chief Exec for...I know what I would choose to do.

(Manager, HR, pay band 8)

IS THIS SUPPORTED BY OTHER RESEARCH?

NHS organisations involve managers from both clinical and general management backgrounds in implementing HR practices. It has been shown that clinical managers struggle to manage the HRM content of their roles and HR managers have been criticised as being distanced from the clinical workforce. Rather than playing a facilitative or advisory role, HR has appeared to play a maintenance role (Fitzgerald, Lillie, Ferlie, Addicott, McGivern and Buchanan, 2006). Some of the findings from this research support this evidence.

Workload

❖ Having too much to do, and pressure from performance targets, were described as key issues, even for managers who were engaged with their HRM role:

Too many things happening at the same time ... Too many targets ... People are not prepared properly for it, or people expect you to know something which you probably don't know.

(Nurse, pay band 7)

❖ Being inexperienced, or lacking confidence, was also seen to have an impact on experiences of role overload, with complaints about being new to the role and feeling out of one's depth due to a lack of training:

New to me. I don't have the qualities of what a line manager should have or the training – so I'm picking it up.

(Administrative, pay band 4)

Confidence in implementing HR policies seemed to be more than just a matter of training, however, but could be attributed to the levels of support for new line managers and previous managerial experience. In particular, this depended, for example, on whether the line manager was initially appointed as a nurse who later became a line manager, or was appointed for managerial skills and was also a nurse.

Q: What happened?
A: There is no management programme. Clinicians don't have people management skills and competencies when they take a management post. You're supposed to gain them – by osmosis.

Q: How did it make you feel?
A: I'm on a hiding to nothing at the moment. That makes me frustrated. These barriers don't need to be put up.

Q: What was the impact on your performance?
A: There are things I need to do and I'm not sure about them – I need to work out how to do it – and that will take time.

Q: How did it affect patient care?
A: Staff need six weeks' notice to attend a training course, but we don't have admin in place to do that. They get held up. If they can't attend eg basic life support management training – which needs to be done annually – it is wasted resources.

(Clinical manager, pay band 8)

HR policies

❖ Policies were associated with a large amount of paperwork. One HR director suggested that this resulted in many managers seeing HR practices as just 'another bit of paperwork or it is another process' that they have to go through. He suggested that improved communication on why a policy has been implemented in the first place was much more important.

With over 300 careers within the NHS, the number of required practices and policies results in a huge amount of regulation and subsequent paperwork to abide by. A number of individuals complained at having to wade through 50 pages to find the information they needed. It is both the number and volume of policies that is problematic, especially at a senior level:

I could fill this room with policy folders. It's trying to get a handle on it, really – key things that have got to be done and that I've really got to know about and what things you can to some extent leave to other people ... It's sheer volume of policies.

(Doctor)

This has resulted in managers having to:

Look them up if you actually just need them ... I can even write policies and not remember what I've written – there are just so many of them.

(Director)

❖ Additional issues relating to policies that were raised included the frequency with which they changed, and the language used. This was stated to be the main constraint in the implementation of policies, with quite a few managers asking for HR policies to be written in language they understand. Front-line managers frequently placed the blame for poorly articulated HR policies on the HR function, whereas the latter complained about the inability to understand HR policies that had been imposed by the Department of Health.

❖ Lack of opportunity to deal with HR issues and policies was suggested by some who reported that because it was rare for them to have to deal with some aspect of HRM, they needed support from more experienced managers and from the HR function when the issue arose.

Appraisal

Despite senior management recognising the importance of HRM, if HRM issues are not included in the appraisal of line managers (see Whittaker and Marchington, 2003), then HRM may not be a priority. This situation was apparent throughout all six case sites, only 37% of line managers reporting that they were appraised on their implementation of HR policies or people management skills. Although appraisals were widespread, specific appraisal about people management issues was less common, although one clinical manager suggested that appraisal covered current managerial concerns:

Oh, say, for example, sickness management – whether we are managing that very well or not, and whether we're managing change very well – so effectively, as much as it affects us, we're appraised on it.

(Nurse, pay band 7)

This research did not consider appraisal systems designed specifically for clinical professionals (eg consultant appraisal) but these appear to be less well accepted and focus on the clinical aspects of the role, in order to support professional revalidation.

> ### IS THIS SUPPORTED BY OTHER RESEARCH?
>
> It has been suggested that effective HRM is the result of discretionary behaviour and personal motivation, rather than organisational assessment (McGovern *et al*, 1997). A lack of institutional pressure to consider HRM results in inconsistencies in implementation (eg Hutchinson and Purcell, 2003; Earnshaw *et al*, 2000).

CONCLUSIONS

Line managers at the case study organisations had developed effective relationships with the HR function, which supported them in carrying out these aspects of their role. The main issues facing line managers when implementing HR policies were concerned with their role, their workload and the policies themselves. Nevertheless, as long as managers fail to be assessed on their managerial skills, HRM will remain a low priority. There is a particular issue for those who have developed into managerial roles from a clinical background, who may choose to prioritise patient care over HRM when they perceive there to be a conflict, in line with their own professional ideology.

What are the links with the rest of the research?

❖ Line managers have an important role in bringing HRM to life and therefore theylink HRM strategy (Chapter 3) to HR practices (Chapter 5).

LEARNING POINTS

❖ HRM is now part of the job for line managers, but there were concerns over the relative priority of HRM compared to other aspects of the role, especially for managers with a clinical background.

❖ The HR function was generally viewed positively in terms of its support for managerial engagement with HRM; it provided specific support and had developed effective relationships with line managers. However, sometimes national initiatives appeared to consume much of its resource.

❖ In practice, involvement in developing HR policies rarely went beyond senior members.

❖ HR policies were perceived as both voluminous and hard to understand.

❖ HR policies were perceived to be too multiplicitous and to change regularly.

❖ Some individuals were relatively inexperienced and lacked confidence in HR issues, particularly where they had a clinical background and no managerial training.

❖ People management issues were rarely directly included in managers' appraisals.

For the organisation as a whole

Effective devolution of responsibility for HRM to clinical and general managers must include recognition of competing priorities and the managerial skills of those managers.

For the HRM system and the HR function

Ensure that the HR function has sufficient capacity to provide support for line managers and establish systems to provide advice for line managers on HRM where this is lacking.

Involve a wider range and level of staff in the development of policies to support people management. This will enable line managers to gain confidence in their understanding of the relevance of policies and how to use them, as well as championing them, and staff to feel that they have ownership of the policies.

Ensure that policies are clear and understandable – think about the language that is used. This applies to the policy itself as well as its rationale, and any guidance on how to implement it.

Exploit the potential of IT to provide summaries and links to detail of policies, as well as ensuring that only the latest version is available.

Train and develop line managers to ensure that they have the knowledge and skills to deal with people management issues.

Develop selection, appraisal and reward processes for line managers (supported by the Knowledge and Skills Framework) that place a priority on their people management skills as well as their operational abilities in meeting organisational goals

HR CONTENT – THE ROLE OF LINE MANAGERS

INDIVIDUALS – THEIR EXPECTATIONS OF WORK

7

✤ **Individuals held various expectations about what they expected their employer would provide for them. These expectations included HR practices, help and encouragement, infrastructure and patient care.**

✤ **Elements of ideological, relational and transactional aspects of the psychological contract of NHS employees and organisations were identified.**

✤ **HRM is important in the management, development and fulfillment of expectations at work.**

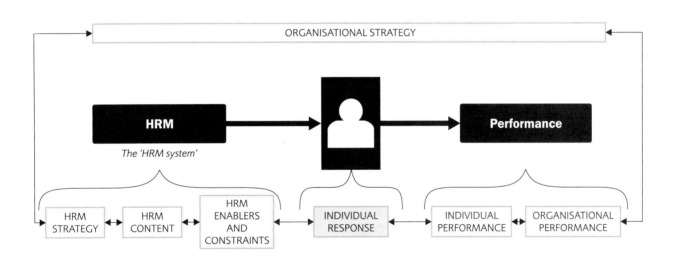

WHAT DOES THIS CHAPTER COVER?

The next two chapters focus on individuals and their responses to HRM. This chapter examines individuals' tacit and explicit expectations of their employer in the following sections:

✤ Meeting expectations: 144 individuals were asked if they had had their expectations at work met

✤ Individual expectations around HR practices

✤ Individual expectations around support and guidance

✤ Individual expectations around infrastructure

✤ Individual expectations around enabling patient care

✤ The impact of having expectations met on patient care.

It is important at the outset to define some key concepts that will be used throughout the chapter.

Key Concept: THE PSYCHOLOGICAL CONTRACT

Psychological contract:

a set of unwritten reciprocal expectations between an individual employee and the organisation

(Schein, 1978; p.48)

The contract has a 'currency' which is the contributions and rewards exchanged in the contract (Thompson and Bunderson, 2003).

LIVERPOOL JOHN MOORES UNIVERSITY
LEARNING SERVICES

There are three aspects of the psychological contract which can be termed three types of 'currency':

❖ *Transactional contracts*, based on an exchange of economic currency

 ❖ The organisation provides pay, and a safe work environment

 ❖ In exchange, the individual fulfils specified role responsibilities.

❖ *Relational contracts*, based on an exchange of socio-emotional currency

 ❖ The organisation provides training and development, as well as long-term job security

 ❖ In exchange the individual fulfils more general role responsibilities (eg commitment to and involvement in the organisation).

❖ *Ideological contracts*, based on an exchange of ideological currency

 ❖ The organisation provides support for a 'cause' or principle valued by the employee (eg resources that advance the cause or promote the cause)

 ❖ In exchange, the individual contributes toward the capacity of the organisation to support the cause (eg taking the initiative to support the cause, acting as an advocate for the cause)

 ❖ Individuals believe that 'the organisation shares my passion, cause and mission' (Thompson and Bunderson, 2003; p.575).

Key Concept: PERFORMANCE

Individual performance can be described using two dimensions.

❖ *Task performance* (also known as *in-role performance*) refers to activities that are formally part of a individual's job and

 ❖ either contribute directly to the technical core (eg operating on patients)

 ❖ or support the technical core (eg hiring individuals) of the organisation.

❖ *Contextual performance* (also known as *extra-role performance*, *pro-social organisational behaviour*, *organisational citizenship behaviour* or *discretionary behaviour*) refers to activities that shape the organisational climate in which the technical core operates. These activities include:

 ❖ persisting with enthusiasm and extra effort as necessary to complete one's own tasks

 ❖ volunteering to carry out task activities that are not formally part of one's own job

 ❖ helping and co-operating with others

 ❖ following organisational rules and procedures

 ❖ endorsing, supporting and defending organisational objectives.

Because the work of some managers does not directly contribute to the technical core, four additional categories represent purely managerial contextual performance (Borman and Motowidlo, 1993, cited in Conway, 1996):

❖ organisational commitment

❖ representing the organisation to customers and public

❖ maintaining good work relationships

❖ persisting to reach goals.

WHAT IS THE CONTEXT?

Although the concept of the psychological contract originates from outside the HRM field, it has nevertheless become a major analytical device in explaining HRM (Cullinane and Dundon, 2006). Despite growing interest in the concept (Turnley and Feldman, 1999), there remains no one universally accepted definition (Anderson and Schalk, 1998). An individual's psychological contract includes combinations of transactional, relational and ideological expectations. In this report we focus specifically on expectations in the workplace. Expectations are shaped by several things:

❖ HRM systems – 'HR practices send strong messages to individuals regarding what the organisation expects of them and what they can expect in return' (Rousseau, 1995; p.162). Rousseau goes on to argue that an organisation's business strategy will determine the type of HRM practices it adopts, and that this in turn has a 'profound impact' on the nature of the psychological contract (Rousseau, 1995, p.185)

❖ individuals within the organisation – HR specialists, direct supervisors and upper-level managers (Turnley and Feldman, 1999)

❖ standard operating practices (and organisational culture) – through observations of organisational practice and socialisation into an organisational culture (Turnley and Feldman, 1999)

❖ individual ideologies – Bunderson (2001) reported two distinct but potentially dual ideologies among doctors: an administrative ideology, represented by delivering efficient services, and a professional ideology characterising the doctor's role as a 'community servant'.

Research has highlighted that the fulfilment of expectations is generally associated with a range of emotional, attitudinal and behavioural consequences, including task performance (eg Lester *et al*, 2002) and contextual performance (eg Othman *et al*, 2005).

WHY IS THIS IMPORTANT?

Understanding what expectations individuals hold in the psychological contract and what they believe the other party expects in return is important in suggesting the role that HRM can play in improving performance, especially in terms of patient care. Although this is not always a direct relationship, it is still important, and where the individual works with patients, or is required to ensure that effective decisions are made, the state of the psychological contract can have more immediate and direct effects on patients. Analysis of tacit expectations shows *why* there were expectations around certain HR practices. Meeting individual expectations is a necessary but not sufficient pre-condition for effective individual performance which may then lead to organisational performance.

WHERE DID THE DATA COME FROM?

We explored individuals' expectations of their employer in two ways:

❖ Individuals were asked directly what they expected from their employers. We have called these *explicit* expectations. They represent the things that are discussed openly from the perspective of individuals.

❖ Individuals were asked about recent incidents where expectations were met and not met. This technique offered the opportunity to tap into implicit aspects of the psychological contract – ie where implicit expectations were exceeded or went unmet. We have called these *tacit* expectations. They represent things that are either so ingrained they have become taken for granted or that the individual values but does not openly discuss.

It should be remembered that individuals were asked about the nature of their expectations *before* they were asked to specifically discuss particular HR practices. Also, because all individuals belong to either high-performing or transformed-performance Trusts, we would expect a relatively high proportion of met expectations. This chapter therefore focuses on *what* expectations are dominant in this context and *how* they may best be characterised.

A total of 152 individuals were asked explicitly what they expected their employer to provide for them. 150 individuals were asked to describe a positive and negative incident at work (incidents accessing tacit expectations) from which tacit expectations were derived. Eleven could not think of a positive incident and 19 could not think of a negative incident. The distribution of responses by job type and grade for both these types of expectations, as compared to the distribution of interview responses in total, is shown in Table 13 below. This suggests that directors and clinical staff were relatively under-represented in the analysis of expectations.

	Total	Job type							Pay band		
		Directors	HR	Clinical	Support	Admin	Hotel	Other	1–4	5–7	8+
Explicit expectations	152	16	19	49	16	38	12	2	55	39	58
Tacit expectations	150	15	19	49	16	37	12	2	54	39	57
Overall total number of interviews	172	22	20	57	18	41	12	2	59	52	61

Table 13 ❖ **Expectations – job types and grades of individuals**

WHAT WERE THE FINDINGS?

Expectations

A total of 354 *explicit expectations* were listed (approximately 2.33 per person). These were divided into four categories: HR practices, help and encouragement, and infrastructure. Patient care expectations were not mentioned explicitly but were seen in the expectations implicit in the critical incidents described. These categories were developed from the data, rather than using a predetermined categorisation.

Although these categories were essentially developed from the data, they did draw on two other categorisations:

Herriot, Manning and Kidd (1997) investigated individual expectations of employers and employer expectations of their employees (although they called them 'obligations'). They report 12 categories for individual expectations of employers:

❖ training

❖ fairness

❖ needs (work–life balance)

❖ consult (communication)

❖ discretion

❖ humanity

❖ recognition

❖ environment

❖ justice

❖ pay

❖ benefits

❖ security

The list of 11 HR practices we had developed earlier in the research (see the section on HRM content in Chapter 2). The only ones from this list not explicitly mentioned as expectations were teamwork and involvement, although it could be argued that 'communication' is a form of involvement. Descriptions of 'support' might however be alternative descriptions of teamwork as support from colleagues was one element mentioned.

Almost half of expectations concerned HR practices, 33% concerned help and encouragement and 22% centred on infrastructure (see Appendix 2, Table 24). There is considerable consistency across sites. For all cases the highest proportion of expectations mentioned was HR practices. However, roughly twice as many individuals voiced expectations about infrastructure (physical environment, social environment, health and safety and resources) in the Primary Care Trust that was being reconfigured (Case 5) than the Primary Care Trust that was not (Case 6).

There are also differences in the expectations that individuals openly voice and those that can be inferred from the critical incidents about work. A total of 270 *tacit expectations* were identified from the incidents: 139 were positive and 131 were negative.

❖ Positive incidents included managerial and collegiate support or recognition, making a difference to patient care, being involved in changes, and HR practices (training, work–life balance and pay).

❖ Negative incidents included lack of managerial and collegiate support or recognition, unmanageable workload, imposed changes, lack of staffing and resources and HR practices (unfair pay, lack of training and poor communication).

In the next sections we summarise the explicit and tacit expectations with regard to each of the four categories: HR practice, help and encouragement, infrastructure and patient care. The explicit expectations are used to help show *what* is important. We use some selective but representative quotes drawn from the narrative (incidents) to characterise *why* these types of expectations were held.

Expectations: HR practices

The most frequently mentioned *explicit* expectations of HR were about training and education (40% of all HR practice expectations mentioned), career (14%), staffing (10%) and pay (8%) (see Appendix 2, Table 25). Expectations about personal development and training reflect that people trade their loyalty for a career in the NHS.

Individuals from all trust types expected training, pay, career development, communication, induction, rewards and adequate levels of staffing. Only a few individuals from the Acute and Mental Health Trusts mentioned appraisal and security. This may reflect the turbulent times in which we conducted the interviews, with primary care staff experiencing job insecurity and little feedback while reorganisations were underway. Work–life balance only featured in half of the sites. The highest proportion of pay and reward expectations were mentioned by Acute Trust staff (the highest proportion in Case 1).

The proportion of explicit expectations relating to HR practices varied across sites. Local context is, then, an important factor in setting HR expectations.

Training featured highly in tacit expectations. Individuals expected access to training that enabled them to do their job.

> There is no management development programme. Clinicians don't have people management skills and competencies when they take up a management post. You're supposed to gain them – by osmosis.

(Clinical manager, pay band 8)

Pay accounted for 8% of explicit expectations. The Agenda for Change pay settlements (Chapter 1) were being agreed at the time of the research and so pay featured as both a positive and a negative experience.

> We got a band 2 instead of a band 3. The forensic unit got a band 3 and we are doing exactly the same.

(Support worker, pay band 2)

A key feature of these experiences revolved around a judgement of fairness.

> Agenda for Change has been a paper exercise. It is supposed to offer fair pay but it doesn't reward experience.

(Nurse, pay band 6)

Tacit expectations of HR also showed the importance of being able to influence changes and get involved in them. A comparison between the positive and negative incidents shows what was important in this. Positive incidents all outlined situations in which individuals had control over how changes were introduced or were involved in changes at work. This included being able to improve systems or develop flexible working arrangements and the opportunity for local improvements to be introduced as individuals utilised their autonomy creatively to improve systems.

> All the beds are full. We have had to bring new wards into being. I have been able to put my ideas forward – where we can fit extra beds in, where we can open other wards.

(Hotel and estates)

Negative incidents outlined situations in which changes to work were perceived as originating from outside the local team or where local views were not canvassed. Individuals did not dispute the need for changes, but felt that if they had been involved a change could have been introduced more successfully.

> The wards had been moved about and we had to go on to Ward 11. There was going to be a cost in bringing the computer down, and therefore – to save costs – we were told we couldn't have the computer.

(Hotel and estates, pay band 5)

These examples illustrate that involvement in change appeared to lead to more positive views of the change and a perception that the change was more successful, whereas lack of involvement was perceived to affect the success of the change.

Expectations: help and encouragement

There are four types of explicit expectation which can be described as 'help and encouragement'. We have developed this typology from descriptions of expectations:

❖ support: socio-emotional support from managers, colleagues

❖ supervision: technical guidance from managers

❖ clarity: a clear understanding of role

❖ leadership: general guidance from managers.

The most frequently mentioned explicit help and encouragement expectations were about support (59% of all expectations mentioned in this area) (see Appendix 2, Table 26). In general, where there are more expectations around the need for support, the need for clarity is not mentioned as much, and vice versa. Individuals from all Trust types expected support, supervision, clarity and leadership.

Help and encouragement also featured as tacit expectations and describe the largest proportion of positive and negative incidents (33%). Support from a manager or colleagues was the most common positive experience, and lack of support or recognition for extra effort was the most frequently reported negative experience. The support of managers was particularly important when individuals were struggling with a work task, whereas recognition was important when individuals had gone above and beyond expectations to reach a deadline or target.

> The consultant I work with is fully supportive. He will praise the team. He will say that he is able to work closely with the team and understands our values. He will seek us out for an opinion on a client – which is very unusual, because normally consultants are a law unto themselves. You enjoy coming to work in the morning.

(Nurse, pay band 6)

Conversely, lack of support from supervisors and colleagues was identified as negative incidents.

> *There was a situation at the last meeting where I think I felt quite exposed and quite belittled in front of the non-exec. It was my [manager] that put me in a very uncomfortable position. I don't think it was intentional but left you feeling quite exposed and almost embarrassed.*

(Director)

Analysis of the ratings of a series of statement by the individuals participating in this research (see Appendix 1) showed that support and impact on others is a two-way thing:

Statement:	1 strongly agree 2 agree 3 not sure 4 disagree 5 strongly disagree	ANOVA (p<.05, two-tailed) Independent samples T-test (p<.05, two-tailed)
I am mindful of how my behaviour affects other people's work	mean score: 1.41 [strongly agree]	❖ Support workers and HR professionals agree more strongly than hotel and estate workers ❖ Females agree more strongly than males

Recognition, for the most part, involved informal thanks for going above and beyond normal duties.

> *We've been through a bit of a change. Our CEO paid me quite a significant compliment about how I had done. I feel more part of the organisation now.*

(Director)

Expectations around help and encouragement were prominent in individuals' accounts of both their *explicit* and their *tacit* expectations: approximately 33% of explicit expectations centred on this (see Appendix 2, Table 24).

Expectations: infrastructure

The most frequently mentioned *explicit* infrastructure expectations were about the physical environment and resources (43% and 44% respectively of all infrastructure expectations mentioned) (see Appendix 2, Table 27).

Expectations about infrastructure reflect the transactional element of the psychological contract to some extent, whereby people require resources to do a job in order to perform well. Individuals from all types of Trust mentioned physical work environment and resources as part of their explicit expectations.

> **Q: What happened?**
> **A:** *We're in a terrible state with the therapy admin. They have put a new computer system in, but quite frankly, it doesn't work. So it takes four times as long as before to book people in for appointments.*
>
> **Q: How did it make you feel?**
> **A:** *Everybody is highly stressed because the admin staff are under enormous pressure. People dread coming to work. You feel so helpless, really, because there is nothing you can do about it.*
>
> **Q: How did it affect patient care?**
> **A:** *Patients can't get through on the phone to make appointments, so there are loads of complaints when they do come to clinic. Patients are normally on three-month return appointments, but they are now going five or six months instead, even though they really need seeing every three months.*

(Support worker, pay band 4)

Infrastructure also featured in *tacit* expectations. Pressures were experienced through staff cuts, with staff shortages more commonly reported by staff on lower pay bands and by clinical and administrative staff. These pressures were linked to low staff morale, uncertainty about the future, and finding work unmanageable, as well as increased stress and sickness absence. Lack of staffing and resources was most commonly reported at Case study 1, but also mentioned at other sites:

> *We are going to cut down on staff, and some staff are going to lose their jobs. The morale in catering is at a low because people don't know what is happening. Morale is low and we are running short-staffed.*

(Hotel and estates, pay band 2)

> **Q: What happened?**
> **A:** *There are a lot of staff cuts – we used to have more staffing. You do challenge why there are more demands put on you and less staff, and ask how you are going to do the same job at the right standard, really. Although people feed that back all the time, you start to think it's not necessarily addressed.*

Q: *How did it make you feel?*
A: *You get frustrated and a bit disheartened, and then you start to think, well, should I move somewhere else? But it's probably the same! You question yourself.*

Q: *What was the impact on your performance?*
A: *If you are tired, you can't concentrate properly – and then you are more likely to forget something or not work as effectively.*

Q: *How did it affect patient care?*
A: *Touch wood – so far I don't think it has. It could have done, but it hasn't. Personally, I've been OK. It's an internal stress, I think. Some staff might go off sick, or they might not deal with a situation as they should do.*

(Therapist, pay band 6)

Individual ratings of a statement about support (which includes but is not limited to physical infrastructure) reinforces this point – although it does show that higher up the organisation there is a stronger belief that appropriate support is provided:

Statement:	1 strongly agree 2 agree 3 not sure 4 disagree 5 strongly disagree	ANOVA (p<.05, two-tailed)
The Trust supports me in providing what I need to do a good job	mean score: 2.30 [agree]	✤ Directors and HR professionals agree more strongly than clinical staff

Clinical managers had particular difficulty in balancing clinical and managerial responsibilities, tending to put clinical duties before managerial work because time for managerial work had been reduced. They described hurrying managerial work to maintain quality of patient care and lacking management skills.

They have taken away a lot of our supernumerary time. So, as a deputy manager we do have a lot of paperwork to do and you can't be out on the shop floor and doing paperwork at the same time. So I am very aware that my paperwork is suffering because I just don't have time to do it. I can get a bit stressed out. You are trying to concentrate on one thing and somebody is calling you out to the floor…When I am actually doing the paperwork, I feel like I am rushing it.

(Nurse, pay band 6)

Expectations: enabling patient care

Although the ability to affect patient care was not explicitly mentioned by individuals, it did feature in individuals' *tacit* expectations, indicating the hidden importance of the 'ideological' element of the psychological contract.

For staff from all organisations and job types, positive incidents concerned situations in which their ability to achieve objectives (ie to 'perform') was recognised. Staff described having a clear idea of what they were setting out to achieve and being able to judge their own success as a result. This 'success' was often concerned with improving services for patients. Although clinical staff may be expected to report making a difference to patients as important to them, these responses came from all staff groups, suggesting core ideologies about providing patient care.

You get a patient home, and you feel that in your team you have achieved for the patient. You get feedback from the family and from the patient themselves about how happy they are with the situation. That's ultimately why we enjoy our job at work – to make the best for the patients. It gets you motivated, and if you get positive feedback, then you know that you are doing the right thing.

(Therapist, pay band 6)

Patient care is obviously a very high priority, and my sort of ethos is that that's what we're here for – for the patient – and we must provide the highest-quality care we can, and the best service we can.

(Clinical manager, pay band 8)

The negative incidents concerned situations that involved perceived reductions in standards of care – complaints from patients and relatives were reported as negative experiences. However, rather than having a negative effect, staff reported learning from the experience and using it to improve patient care in the future.

Dealing with patient complaints … I'm always disappointed – but it's how you deal with it and how you get your staff to learn from it. We take time out to look at the care being provided and to ensure that patients' needs are being met.

(Nurse, pay band 8)

How do met expectations impact on patient care?

In Chapter 9 we explore what individuals understand about the nature of performance and whether this understanding bears any relation or not to organisational performance, or to their own individual perspective. However, it is important here to consider whether the meeting of employee expectations matters or not in terms of performance, described here as patient care. We have already shown that over 70% of individuals reported having their expectations met at work. Do individuals *believe* that there is any consequence for patient care or not? If they do, whether or not evidence actually bears this out, this belief will govern their receptiveness to change.

Individuals were asked in open interview whether, on the whole, their expectations had been met at work, then whether the meeting of their expectations impacted on their performance, and then on patient care. Almost three-quarters of individuals felt that having their *explicit* expectations met impacted on the delivery of patient care. In high-performing and transformed-performance Trusts this, reassuringly, is to be expected. The examples given of what constituted patient care and the mechanisms that influenced it are explored further in Chapter 9. However, the meeting of expectations was seen as mutually reinforcing:

> We've got expectations about being able to do our job with the clients and the patients, so if ours are being met, we can meet the expectations that they've got of us as well.

(Support worker, pay band 2)

CONCLUSIONS

Expectations at work can be both explicit (ie openly discussed) and tacit (ie taken for granted or not openly discussed). A high proportion of individuals reported having their explicit expectations met at work. These expectations centred around HR practices, help and encouragement, infrastructure, and patient care:

❖ HR practices – Individuals mentioned a range of expectations around specific HR practices. Some reflected the transactional nature of the psychological contract (eg adequate pay) while others reflected its relational nature (eg training and personal development).

❖ help and encouragement – Individuals mentioned a range of expectations around the need for support, clarity, leadership and supervision. The importance of recognition was also highlighted. These expectations reflected relational aspects of the psychological contract.

❖ infrastructure – Individuals mentioned a range of expectations around physical environment, social environment, health and safety, resources and time. These reflected transactional elements of the psychological contract (eg adequate staffing).

❖ enabling patient care – This was a tacit expectation and related to the opportunity and support to deliver excellent patient care. It reflects the ideological aspect to the psychological contract.

Individuals articulated a connection between met expectations and the delivery of patient care.

What are the links with the rest of the research?

❖ Individual expectations are influenced by HRM content – specifically HR practices (Chapter 5).

❖ They are also influenced by enablers and constraints to the implementation of HRM (Chapter 6).

❖ It will also be shown that having expectations met has an influence on individual performance (Chapter 9) – often through a mediating emotional response.

LEARNING POINTS

❖ Individuals hold a range of expectations about what their employer should provide for them.

The organisation must understand what these expectations are: many concern HR practices and other aspects of the employment relationship that the HR function can play a role in (ie HRM engagement with staff), but others have wider implications.

❖ Individual expectations appeared to vary depending on case site – indicating that local context may shape people's expectations.

The organisation must ensure that it sends out consistent messages regarding what people can expect. This will involve HRM systems, policies and procedures as well as other management processes.

❖ It is clear that individuals felt that their tacit expectations were met when they were involved in the process of change, and that this led to improved performance.

As the organisation changes, individuals have to be supported to adjust their expectations. Being honest and keeping people involved and informed will help this – and there is a role here for the HR function to support engagement with staff.

❖ Individual expectations around support and encouragement were often met through communication, not only from the HR function but also from others in the team or management structure.

Enabling and encouraging a supportive workplace for all staff should be a priority for the organisation and is not simply the responsibility of the HR function.

❖ The ideological aspects of the psychological contract were evident in tacit expectations of being enabled to provide patient care.

The professionalism of NHS staff must be clearly understood and supported if performance is to be sustained – this is something which makes the NHS different from other types of organisation.

❖ Infrastructure, especially staffing levels, was often not perceived as being aligned with organisational goals or the way that they are translated into the demands of individual jobs.

Infrastructure should be aligned with work/role requirements, since a lack of alignment leads to weakened performance.

For the HRM system and the HR function

❖ Explicit expectations of various HR practices varied across sites.

It is therefore important that HR understands the expectations employees hold of HR practices rather than assuming a particular set of expectations.

INDIVIDUALS – PERCEPTIONS OF EMPLOYER EXPECTATIONS

8

❖ **Most individuals thought their employers expected task performance: getting the job done.**

❖ **Colleagues and team-work were important in enabling individuals to meet employer expectations, having too much to do being the main constraint.**

❖ **Going beyond employer expectations – contextual performance – was most commonly described in terms of staying later at work than planned or expected. This was generally linked to, and motivated by, patient care.**

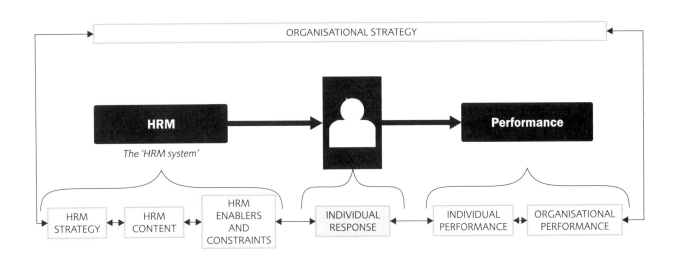

WHAT DOES THIS CHAPTER COVER?

The previous chapter described individual expectations in the NHS. However, a healthy psychological contract results from an individual and an organisation achieving mutually beneficial working arrangements. This chapter explores the relationship between employer expectations and individual willingness to go beyond these expectations in five sections:

❖ Employers' expectations (as perceived by individuals)

❖ Helping individuals to meet their employers' expectations

❖ Constraints in meeting employers' expectations

❖ Contextual performance

❖ The links between 'going beyond' and patient care.

WHAT IS THE CONTEXT?

We outlined the context of psychological contracts in the previous chapter and discussed the expectations of individuals. This chapter focuses on what individuals assume is expected of them in return.

WHY IS THIS IMPORTANT?

The importance of understanding these assumed employer expectations is that it enables policy-makers to understand the interpretation of the policy 'messages' that are currently being sent about the nature of performing in the NHS, and how they are interpreted within organisations. Does the workforce have a realistic and informed view of what is important? Is there line of sight between what they see as effective individual performance and appropriate organisational outcomes? How

Table 14 ❖ Employer expectations – number of individuals

Case	Total	Directors	HR	Clinical	Support	Admin	Hotel	Other	1–4	5–7	8+
1	11	1	1	3	0	1	5	0	5	2	4
2	24	3	4	9	0	7	1	0	7	6	11
3	23	1	5	6	5	6	0	0	10	7	6
4	28	5	1	10	3	7	2	0	9	9	10
5	23	2	0	8	5	5	2	1	10	6	7
6	26	2	6	8	1	9	0	0	8	8	10
Total	135	14	17	44	14	35	10	1	49	38	48

can individual expectations and needs be aligned with the true organisational requirements?

Assessing perceived employer expectations is not a measure of what is actually asked by employers, but it does assess the message received by individuals. If there is a mismatch between perceived expectation and official policy, then either policy is not sensitive to the realities of work, or individuals conceive of work in ways that are too constrained. However, given the range of occupational groups covered in this research, and the complex range of stakeholder views about what constitutes performance, we would expect some level of mismatch between perceived employer expectations and expectations intended by the employer.

WHERE DID THE DATA COME FROM?

In the previous chapter we detailed how individuals were asked about what they expected their employers to provide for them. Individuals were also asked what they thought their employer expected from them. 135 individuals were asked what they thought their employer expected of them (see Table 14 above).

WHAT WERE THE FINDINGS?

We based our categorisation on that developed by Herriot, Manning and Kidd (1997), who report seven categories for employer expectations of individuals:

❖ hours

❖ work

❖ honesty

❖ loyalty

❖ property

❖ self-presentation (professionalism)

❖ flexibility.

Employers' expectations of their staff

A total of 181 *explicit* expectations were listed (approximately 1.34 per person). These included:

❖ functional commitment: 'I suppose they expect me to meet my job description, basically' (Nurse, pay band 8)

❖ honesty: '… ability to be open and honest' (Administrative, pay band 4)

❖ reliability: 'reliable, punctual, know my limitations, competent' (Nurse, pay band 8)

❖ professionalism: 'run a professional service' (Administrative, pay band 5)

❖ property: 'not to abuse any of their procedures' (Support worker, pay band 2)

❖ flexibility: 'job description, annual appraisals. But that's the "day job". That's what [I'm] expected to do, but what I think my employer's got the right to expect, and what I believe my job's really about, is managing those things that come out of the blue' (Director)

❖ loyalty: 'I think it expects you to be committed' (Nurse, pay band 8)

❖ targets/objectives: 'that the hospital runs and that all the targets are met in terms of the performance measures' (Director)

❖ leadership: '...expecting leadership, direction, a vision for the future' (Nurse, pay band 8)

❖ don't know – some individuals do not have a view of what is expected of them: 'That's difficult because I don't know at the moment – I'm in between roles' (Administrative, pay band 3).

Almost two-thirds of perceived employer expectations were about getting one's job done (functional commitment) and 14% were about being professional (see Appendix 2, Table 28). One implication of these task-oriented expectations is that when times change, people's expectations have to be renegotiated to the extent that their job and role changes. Generally, expecting people to be flexible in times of change may also be more difficult because people have very set task expectations – any attempt to change the nature of an individual's work may be perceived as a breach of the psychological contract.

Because of the range of local expectations different Trusts may have of their individuals, it is important to explore whether there were differences in answers given at each Trust. Interestingly, getting the job done was mentioned more frequently at Cases 1 and 5. In addition, targets and objectives were mentioned more frequently by individuals from Case 1. This suggests that individuals at different case sites have differing perceptions of what they believe their employer expects from them, again indicating the importance of local context in shaping expectations.

Task orientation

Individuals had a largely task-oriented view of what their employers expected of them. In an organisation like the NHS that involves the levels of risk associated with clinical work, it is important that individuals do not go beyond what is expected of them where this relates to technical aspects of the role that require a certain level of skill and experience. Within a culture that does not encourage risk-taking due to clinical governance requirements and regulation, it is hardly surprising that we found that individuals largely believed their employers expected them to do the job as specified. Professional roles are perhaps more tightly defined than some other types.

This task-orientation could make it more difficult to change organisations because it will involve not only renegotiation of roles, but also changes to the requirements of role specified by external professional regulation.

Enabling individuals to meet employer expectations

We also asked individuals what helps them to meet (what we call 'enablers') their employers' expectations. A total of 127 enablers were listed (see Appendix 2, Table 29). These included:

❖ HRM (training and development, feedback and appraisal, communication and information): 'Keep updated – go on courses' (Nurse, pay band 5)

❖ team/colleague: 'Well, it is team-work, isn't it? Really, if your team is working properly and everything is running smoothly, then you can get on with your job. It is all down to team-work in here' (Hotel and estates, pay band 3)

❖ manager (having someone to bounce ideas off and someone to stick up for you): 'Good support from manager' (Nurse, pay band 7)

❖ autonomy: 'Externally, yeah, I have a lot of freedom, I think – a lot of trust. I have a lot of freedom to do things that other organisations, or other bosses or other groups of directors might not tolerate' (HR professional, pay band 8)

❖ resources: 'I suppose, practically, IT has been a real boon to people like me' (Director)

❖ culture/image: 'This organisation is really positive about what can be done' (HR professional, pay band 8)

❖ policies: 'Just keeping on top of new [policies] coming out, really, and for me with any of the ones that have been a long time around as well' (Support worker, pay band 2)

❖ self: 'I organise myself' (Doctor).

The most frequently mentioned items that helped individuals meet employer expectations for all cases were colleagues/team and relationships at work (29%), HRM (18%) and support from managers (12%) (see Appendix 2, Table 29).

IS THIS SUPPORTED BY OTHER RESEARCH?

Relationships at work appear to be a key factor in enabling individuals to meet their employers' expectations. This is consistent with previous research in the NHS on team-work (West et al, 2002, 2006) and line manager engagement (Purcell et al, 2003) and also with individuals' expectations of their employer.

Constraints in meeting expectations

We also asked individuals what hinders them from meeting their employers' expectations. A total of 115 constraints were listed. These included:

❖ workload demands – lack of time, too much paperwork/administration, too much to do: 'I mean, the thing that hinders me – probably the thing that hinders me most – is time and just basically running out of time' (Doctor); 'Enormous amount of monitoring and reporting. It takes a huge chunk of time. It is a significant diversion. It irritates me, really' (Clinical manager, pay band 8); 'Demands of individuals far greater these days. That hinders you' (Administrative, pay band 4)

❖ manager/colleague: 'Other heads of department not feeding back, emails getting ignored about important things, general organisation of the people' (HR professional, pay band 5)

❖ HR practices (lack of security, lack of communication, difficulties balancing work and home life): 'Difficult to do everything in role and balance with young family' (HR professional, pay band 8)

❖ external demands (too many of them): 'I think the constraints are usually simply external factors, whether it be Department of Health policy agendas, the Strategic Health Authority wanting reports, and returns' (Director)

❖ environment: 'Open-plan working can have an adverse effect, I think' (Administrative, pay band 8)

❖ lack of staff/of resources: 'Compared to my colleagues around the ward: they all have what you call a ward clerk to assist them with administrative tasks – and I don't have that' (Nurse, pay band 7)

❖ administrative issues: 'Decision-making within the organisation. I think decision-making at the top is sometimes lacking' (Manager, pay band 7)

❖ self: 'I say things without thinking, sometimes' (Administrative, pay band 2)

❖ other: 'Age issues' (HR professional, pay band 8)

❖ nothing.

The most frequently mentioned constraint to meeting employer expectations was workload demand – ie a lack of time/too much paperwork/having too much to do (24%) (see Appendix 2, Table 30). This workload demand was attributed to a number of sources:

❖ government initiatives: 'There are lots of things that the government have brought in about knowledge, skills and framework, and all these other things which in a sense piles more paperwork on you' (Hotel and estates, pay band 3)

❖ procedures: 'I am not a paperwork shuffler, I must admit, but we are taking up too much time with practitioners doing it. Why don't we look at the paperwork we are doing?' (Nurse, pay band 6)

❖ volume of work: 'Busy wards. Being overwhelmed with patients' (Doctor).

In summary, colleagues and team-work were the most mentioned enablers of meeting employer expectations, highlighting the importance of good relationships at work. Having too much to do was a constraint on meeting employer expectations and was linked to paperwork, procedures and volume of work.

IS THIS SUPPORTED BY OTHER RESEARCH?

It is important to recognise that unmet expectations do not always result in reduced effort and performance. The extent to which individuals believe that their expectations have not been met because of intent or some other uncontrollable factors will affect their reactions. The important feature is in maintaining congruence between individual and organisational expectations (Robinson and Morrison, 2000).

When do individuals 'go beyond' what they think their employer expects?

Individuals were each asked to give one example of a time when they had gone beyond their employer's expectations. This generated a total of 142 such examples (1 per individual). These were analysed according to Borman and Motowidlo's (1993) contextual performance categories as far as possible, since 'going beyond' one's employer's expectations may represent times when people engage in contextual performance (see Appendix 2, Table 31).

IS THIS SUPPORTED BY OTHER RESEARCH?

Our exploration of contextual performance stems from the belief that these behaviours do indeed contribute to organisational performance. For example, helping new colleagues to 'learn the ropes' enables them to come up to speed quicker with a task and be productive more quickly; picking up the slack when colleagues are absent may enhance the stability of a team's performance. Empirical research shows that in particular 'helping others' is associated with enhanced organisational performance quality and quantity (Podsakoff and MacKenzie, 1997).

We used a 'bottom-up' approach to develop the categories used here, but three of Borman and Motowidlo's (1993) categories were also incorporated to categorise examples of going beyond one's employer's expectations:

❖ persisting

❖ volunteering

❖ helping.

Individuals also reported examples associated with working extra hours (hours), and doing more work than one gets paid for (work). Some individuals did not think anything that they did was beyond their employer's expectations (nothing is beyond). The 'other' category contained many idiosyncratic examples that were hard to characterise under one label.

❖ Hours (25%): 'Any time you stay late, really, is *more* than what is expected of you.' (Doctor)

❖ Helping (9%): 'Sorting out the patient's funeral for her family.' (Support worker, pay band 2)

❖ Persisting (5%): 'If I'm having a problem with A&E and I've got beds and we're not meeting the government target here in terms of the patients, then I'll go beyond the SHO. I will probably ring the registrar, and if nothing is done, I will ring the consultant himself – I will push.' (Nurse, pay band 5)

❖ Volunteering (16%): 'Sometimes I do things that I am not banded for, like taking minutes at a meeting.' (Administrative, pay band 2)

❖ Work (7%): 'Nothing specific, just helping patients.' (Support worker, pay band 2)

Q: What have you done that you think is 'going beyond' what your employer expects?
A: *I work on a ward, and a patient was due to be transferred out of the hospital. A wheelchair had been booked but the patient was too poorly and needed a stretcher. There was a new nurse who really didn't know how to go about things, so I had to cancel the ambulance because it was only suitable for wheelchairs. When I explained it to the nurse, he realised that 'Oh yes, this patient*

needs a stretcher.' That went beyond my role, really, because I shouldn't really do that.

Q: Why did you do it?
A: *I just felt I had to do it, really. And I had to act really fast.*

Q: How did it make you feel?
A: *I was very frustrated to know that the patient was supposed to be going out in a wheelchair – but he can't even sit in a wheelchair for 30 minutes. It made me feel really stressed at that time. Am I doing the right thing? Am I going to get into trouble?*

Q: How did it affect patient care?
A: *The patient was very happy that I made that decision because he felt that, 'Oh, God, I would have had to get into the wheelchair!' The ambulance drivers were thankful as well because they said they would have been stressed on the ambulance because they weren't paramedics or anything.*

(Support worker, pay band 2)

Staying late at work longer than expected by employers was mentioned by many individuals – but not the majority – as an example of going beyond expectations. It is important that individuals do not continually work longer hours than expected because it has been associated with various symptoms of poor health (Sparks *et al*, 1997) and accidents at work (Folkard and Lombardi, 2006) as well as risking patient safety (Rogers *et al*, 2004).

In 9% of the examples there was a simple attitude expressed that *nothing* is beyond expectations. Approximately two thirds of individuals that reported that 'nothing is beyond' were directors.

It doesn't feel like an extra mile. It is what you accept as part of the job. If on a Saturday afternoon the telephone rings because there is an issue to deal with, you just do that. I don't think you would find a member of the executive who wouldn't 99% of the time be available seven days a week, 24 hours a day, 365 days of the year. That is just the way we operate because there is that tremendous commitment, that real sense of belonging to this organisation – and if it needs you, then it gets you. On occasions that would mean that you roll your sleeves up and get your hands dirty.

(Director)

For directors and higher-pay-banded individuals, 'doing whatever is necessary' may seem to be part of one's job. This might explain why it was mainly directors and higher-pay-banded individuals who thought that 'nothing was beyond' expectations.

INDIVIDUALS – PERCEPTIONS OF EMPLOYER EXPECTATIONS

Why is contextual performance so important?

According to Borman and Motowidlo (1993) contextual performance can be classified as:

* persisting with enthusiasm to reach goals

* volunteering to carry out tasks that are not part of one's role

* helping and co-operating with others and maintaining good work relationships

* following rules and sustaining commitment

* representing the organisation and defending organisational objectives.

In the above examples, some areas were seen as drawing unnecessarily on goodwill whereas others were freely contributed. It is interesting that although individuals willingly contribute caring activity and persistence against bureaucracy, they felt that staying late exceeded expectations. This may be a product of the task orientation of individuals noted in the previous chapter. It may also reflect the unpredictable nature of work in the NHS.

Why do individuals 'go beyond'?

As noted above, sometimes 'going beyond' is a more willing activity than at other times. We asked individuals what encouraged them to go beyond expectations. A total of 135 reasons were given for (willingly) going beyond employers' expectations. These included:

* Self (31%): 'My curiosity, my questioning, and not being able to get the answers.' (HR professional, pay band 5)

* The demands of the job (21%): 'Sometimes you have no choice – it's not working – because sometimes people say it's bad time management. But it's not – it's because something has cropped up and you have to deal with it.' (Therapist, pay band 6)

* Colleagues (17%): 'The team in here, I think, because I know it's not just me. I think most people would. They do chop and change, and lots of things probably come to me when I'm out there. It's a good and friendly team.' (Nurse, pay band 5)

* Patient (11%): 'The patient should receive the best possible service.' (Radiographer, pay band 6)

* Managerial recognition (3%): 'If I have gone that extra mile, there will always be a thank you from the Chief Executive or from the Chair for doing that.' (Director).

Q: **What have you done that you think is 'going beyond' what your employer expects?**

A: *I've been to the chemist's for patients [in the community] because they haven't got anyone to fetch their medication for them.*

Q: **Why did you do it?**

A: *Because I want to do the best for the patients and I want to be human. Unless you are human there is no point in you being in the NHS.*

Q: **How did it make you feel?**

A: *Like I was doing a good job.*

Q: **How did it affect patient care?**

A: *They got their medication all right.*

(Therapist, pay band 7)

Q: **What have you done that you think is 'going beyond' what your employer expects?**

A: *I work in a staff bank office. We had a very late staff cancellation on a qualified shift due to a broken-down vehicle. Our office hours are 8 to 6, but I agreed to stay and let the other colleague go home until the on-call service arrived. I stayed until quarter to seven and managed to fill that post and dealt with it.*

Q: **Why did you do it?**

A: *Other staff sometimes cover for us. In this environment there are awkward wards – for example, elderly wards with senile dementia and Alzheimer's – and sometimes you have got to encourage staff that work on acute wards or forensic wards to stand in and help us fill that shift.*

Q: **How did it affect patient care?**

A: *The knock-on effect [of not covering for others in this way] is that the wards are understaffed and that the service-user isn't going to get the appropriate care they need.*

(Clerical, pay band 2)

There was some ambivalence about whether extra effort was appreciated, although HR staff felt more strongly that it was appreciated compared to clinical and hotel and estates staff:

Statement:	1 strongly agree 2 agree 3 not sure 4 disagree 5 strongly disagree	ANOVA (p<.05, two-tailed)
The Trust fails to appreciate any extra effort from me	mean score: 3.24 [not sure]	❖ HR professionals disagree more strongly than clinical and hotel and estates staff

Of the examples of going beyond employer expectations, 7% of individuals concerned argued that going beyond was just part of the culture; 6% gave idiosyncratic reasons; and 4% did not offer a reason.

In sum, over a third of individuals reported that they went beyond what their employer expected of them of their own volition. Others reported that they did it to support colleagues, or to deliver patient care. Only about a fifth reported that it was due to the demands of the job. This implies that jobs should be designed in a way that individuals can achieve what is expected of them in a reasonable time.

IS THIS SUPPORTED BY OTHER RESEARCH?

According to Borman and Motowidlo (1993), variation in task performance is a function of ability, knowledge and skills, whereas variation in contextual performance is a function of volition and personality. Consistent with Borman and Motowidlo, a third of individuals suggested that going beyond their employers' expectations was down to their own volition.

The effects of 'going beyond' on patient care

Around 80% of individuals who reported going the extra mile also reported that they felt that by doing so they had made an impact on patient care. Examples that individuals from a range of occupational groups used to illustrate this are shown in the quotes below.

Q: *What have you done that you think is 'going beyond' what your employer expects?*
A: *When you're on your own in clinic and there's supposed to be two or three of you. This morning, we'd got people off sick.*

Q: *Why did you do it?*
A: *Can't predict people being off sick, so you get on with it. Patient care, really. If I'm not there, they won't get seen. My team are very supportive. We all pull together.*

Q: *How did it affect patient care?*
A: *[If you don't do it,] patients wouldn't get seen. You do your best, but you are limited. You have to prioritise a bit more than you usually do.*

(Therapist, pay band 7)

Q: *What have you done that you think is 'going beyond' what your employer expects?*
A: *We've had quite a lot of different managers, and some managers – because they were put into acting roles – they were quite inexperienced, so I've felt then that I've gone further than I perhaps normally would to assist them. I suppose because of the length of time I've been here!*

Q: *Why did you do it?*
A: *Well, you just want the service to run properly. You just want to make sure that everything is being done properly.*

Q: *How did it affect patient care?*
A: *Well, indirectly, I suppose it would. If we were making sure that everything was done properly, it's got to have an effect on the patient care – and that has got to be kept to a high standard for the patient.*

(Administrative, pay band 5)

In the following example, the individual takes care to check that volunteering is not something that will be of detriment to patient care, by limiting the volunteering to patients who are on a normal diet rather than ones with swallowing problems, for whom more specialised help would be needed.

Q: What have you done that you think is 'going beyond' what your employer expects?

A: I did ask once if I could feed the patients because they were really short ... Someone from higher up (I can't remember who) said I could, as long as I felt comfortable – if I didn't feel comfortable, then don't do it. I never feed a patient who has got swallowing problems or anything like that. I just feed people who are on a normal diet but they can't feed themselves. I'm quite comfortable with that – it doesn't bother me.

Q: Why did you do it?

A: When we've got time, I'll say 'Can I feed somebody?' and they're quite happy with that – and I'm quite happy with that. I always say to them, 'You help us and we'll help you,' and we work as a team. It's nice for me to show that I care. And I think we're all going to get old, and I'm only doing for them what I'd like somebody to do for me when I get older.

Q: How did it affect patient care?

A: Nobody wants to eat a cold dinner!

(Hotel and estates, pay band 2)

CONCLUSIONS

The majority of responses centred on getting the job done and may reflect the professional ideology that doing one's job contributes to patient care. The majority of responses about enablers to meeting employer expectations focused on colleagues and team-work. This fits with individuals' expectations of their employer, in that support from colleagues and managers was the most mentioned *tacit* expectation and the second most mentioned *explicit* expectation. Having too much to do was the most commonly cited reason for not being able to fulfil one's employer's expectations.

Staying late was the most commonly mentioned example of going beyond expectations – although this was not by the majority of the individuals interviewed – and it was reported that this was most often because of personal preference. Individuals perceived that there was a link between contextual performance and the outcome of patient care. Other examples of going beyond expectations covered a wide range of areas, being most commonly driven by what the individual wanted to do himself or herself, and often by wanting to support colleagues. It is clear that individuals understood that the NHS expects them to go beyond what they perceive as the expectations of the employer when it is safe and reasonable to do so, and when individuals are competent to do it.

Although these findings illustrate how individuals contribute to the performance of the organisation as a whole, they do not illustrate a direct line of sight between individual and organisational performance outcomes. The next chapter explores links between individual and organisational performance.

LEARNING POINTS

❖ Most individuals reported that they were enabled to meet the expectations of their employer because of colleagues and team-work.

❖ This research shows that staff are generally willing to go beyond expectations, especially where there would otherwise be a detrimental impact on patient care.

❖ A small proportion of senior staff believed that nothing was beyond expectations.

❖ Individuals reported going beyond employer expectations in terms of working extra hours or doing more work than they were paid for (contextual performance).

❖ Research has shown that working long hours over a sustained period has detrimental effects on individual health and safety at work.

❖ Having too much to do constrained individuals in achieving employer expectations.

❖ Most individuals believe that their employer expects them to get their job done – a task-oriented view of their work.

For the organisation as a whole

Organisations must encourage effective teamworking as well as provide opportunities for colleagues to support each other informally.

The development of understanding about *why* and *when* individuals go beyond expectations is needed. If this then highlights any underlying system issues, these must be resolved at that point. There may be a role for the HR function in this.

It is vital that this is not detrimental to the overall work–life balance of these individuals, or to the organisation as a whole. The boundaries of every job – even those of senior managers – should be set so they are reasonable; otherwise, there is a risk of burnout.

It is also important that the view that 'nothing is beyond expectations' is not promoted as an example of how work should be done (even indirectly) because this could lead to a bullying culture.

The organisation must ensure it is acceptable to discuss volume and content of work.

For the HRM system and the HR function

The long-term implications of working long hours over a sustained period should be communicated to individuals, and support given to them to address the issue. Line managers are important in this process.

Ensure that the workload is appropriate and that jobs are designed in a way that means that individuals do not routinely have to work extra hours.

Ensure that teamwork is effective in supporting individuals when they have issues of workload. Line managers are important in this process.

HRM must ensure that the demands of the job are realistic and that individuals understand these demands. This will then avoid detrimental effects on individuals or others in their team.

PERFORMANCE IN THE NHS – INDIVIDUALS AND ORGANISATIONS

9

❖ **Individual performance is influenced by professional ideology and emotions – and by external factors: training, infrastructure, help and encouragement from others and feedback on performance.**

❖ **Organisational performance is assessed using 'targets' for aspects of the process of care, seen at times to be in conflict with patient care.**

❖ **Organisational and individual performance were linked through use of resources and patient care.**

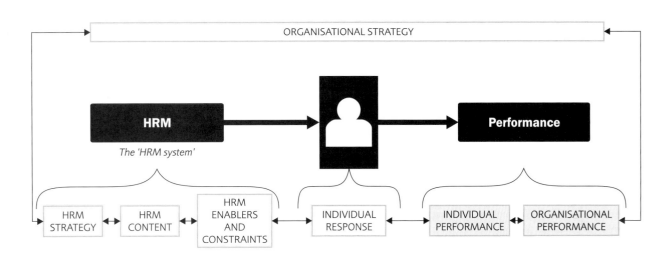

WHAT DOES THIS CHAPTER COVER?

The chapter covers the following areas:

❖ how individuals perceive their performance, including both technical and interpersonal aspects of care

❖ how individuals thought organisations performed in terms of the process of care. This includes some discussion about the role of 'targets' in providing patient care, and the issues of technical and interpersonal quality of care at an organisational level. The perceived differences between performance at an organisational and the NHS level are also discussed

❖ how individuals thought organisations performed in terms of outcomes for patients

❖ the factors common to descriptions of performance at the NHS, organisational and individual levels, and the way in which these levels may be linked.

The term 'performance' is not a single concept – it has multiple meanings. There are a variety of concepts used to describe performance in this chapter.

Key Concept: PERFORMANCE – THE PROCESS OF CARE

The process of care is the 'interactions between users and the health care structure' (Campbell *et al*, 2000) – ie the actual delivering and receiving of care. The process comprises both technical and interpersonal elements:

❖ *technical* – the application of professional knowledge and skills to a 'personal health problem' (Campbell *et al*, 2000). This should be both appropriate and necessary. Some authors term this the 'clinical' element of the process (Campbell *et al*, 2000)

❖ *interpersonal* – the interaction of healthcare professionals and patients (and carers): 'the management of the social and psychological interaction' (Donabedian, 1980; p.5). In this research the term 'patient care' was often used by individuals when discussing what can be defined as the interpersonal aspects of the process of healthcare provision.

Key Concept: PERFORMANCE – THE OUTCOME OF CARE

The outcome is the consequences of care – involving social and psychological function as well as patient attitudes (including satisfaction). The main measures of outcome are:

❖ *health status* – eg blood sugar level

❖ *user evaluation* – eg satisfaction, enablement and health-related quality of life. These are associated with patient expectation too.

Key Concept: PATIENT CARE

Patient care was widely reported by individuals as a key element of their individual performance, and of organisational performance, but is not widely used in literature. We use the term 'patient care' to refer to the process of care provided for the patient, while acknowledging that this is a term with multiple meanings (Klein *et al*, 1961):

Patient care, like morale, cannot be considered as a unitary concept ... It seems likely that there will never be a single comprehensive criterion by which to measure the quality of patient care.

Key Concept: ORGANISATIONAL AND INDIVIDUAL PERFORMANCE

An alternative way in which to view performance is to consider the various levels at which performance is assessed – from the NHS as a whole through organisations and groups/teams down to each individual employee.

Measures of organisational performance increasingly include non-financial measures, and frameworks such as the 'balanced scorecard' have become increasingly popular (Kaplan and Norton, 1996) so that 'outcome measures and the performance drivers of outcomes, linked together in cause–effect relationships' (Norreklit, 2000) can be demonstrated. This research does not explicitly consider performance at group/team level.

At the individual level of performance, there is a wide range of literature covering a number of constructs, including the concepts of task and contextual performance (see Chapter 7).

WHAT IS THE CONTEXT?

Commonly used models for assessing performance in public services include the 3Es model (economy, efficiency and effectiveness) (Boyne, 2002b) and the input-outputs-outcomes model. However, in this research we have used elements of a framework originally developed for the assessment of the quality of health care (Donabedian, 1980) – the structure-process-outcome model – on the basis that 'good performance' equates with 'high quality of care'. This model is similar to those used for assessing service quality which distinguishes between the process and the outcome (Johnson and Clark, 2005; and Chapter 1).

This research focuses on the process of care for an individual rather than for a whole population, because of our focus on single organisations which on their own cannot easily influence population health outcomes.

The overall research objective can also be framed in terms of the model proposed by Donabedian (1980) who precedes consideration of process and outcome by defining structure, and its relationship to process and outcome:

STRUCTURE

The 'organisational factors that define the healthcare system under which care is provided' (Donabedian, 1980). These characteristics can be divided into:

❖ physical – which include resources, the way they are organised and managed

❖ staff – which include skill mix and teamworking.

Structure is essentially relatively stable and relevant to quality (and therefore to performance) in that 'it increases or decreases the probability of good performance' (Donabedian, 1980; p.82) (see also Chapter 2).

The structural characteristics of the settings in which care takes place have a propensity to influence the process of care ... Changes in the process of care ... will influence the effect of care on health status, broadly defined'.

(Donabedian, 1980; p.84)

Whether there is a cause–effect relationship between structure, process and outcome is, however, more debatable, in line with evidence about the relationship between HRM and performance (Hyde *et al*, 2006a):

❖ Some aspects of structure (including those associated with HRM) lead to more effective technical quality, others to interpersonal, with some factors interacting to affect both (Flood, 1994; Laschinger *et al*, 2001).

❖ The relationship between health system effectiveness (ie process) and improved health outcomes 'remains unsettled' (Arah *et al*, 2003; p.392).

❖ Although the evidence appears to be mixed, it is often positive (Lilford *et al*, 2004).

This focus on both process and outcome is summarised by a NHS Chief Executive asked to describe 'customer focus' :

It's hard to define and hard to measure. There are two elements:

❖ *the patient's experience – 'What did it feel like? How was I treated?'*

❖ *the outcome – 'Did I get better? Did something go wrong?'*

They are connected but separate – the question is how we achieve both.

David Fillingham, Bolton Hospitals NHS Trust
in NHS Confederation (2007a; p.6)

WHY IS THIS IMPORTANT?

Just as the earlier chapters of this report have explored and deepened the understanding of what 'HRM' is and the dynamics of its implementation within organisations, and its impact on individuals, so the understanding of 'performance' must be deepened.

By conceptualising healthcare as the provision of a service, the process view enables the distinction to be made between performance in terms of the process of care as distinct from the changes in outcome for the patient on whom the process of healthcare is performed. If the concept of technical and interpersonal performance in terms of process is also included, this gives further insight into the dynamics of performance. Individuals within the healthcare organisation (and other partners involved in providing care) are part of the process, and it is the 'performance' of the process which leads to improved outcomes for patients.

WHERE DID THE DATA COME FROM?

We gathered performance data from a variety of sources throughout the research. Previous work has highlighted the lack of use of objective sources of performance data (Boselie *et al*, 2005; p.76): 'many of the studies had to rely on managers' perceptual estimates.' In this study we utilise both sources in terms of organisational performance, with objective data about performance from external ratings summarised in Chapter 3. The data in this chapter is from comments made by individuals and therefore might be considered subjective.

A question was asked of all individuals specifically about what they thought performance was, in terms of the NHS as a whole, of their organisation and of their own role. Accounts of positive and negative incidents also contained information about how individuals perceived performance in their own role, and the impact of these positive and negative incidents on performance in terms of patient care. Descriptions of what it meant to go beyond expectations, as well as data on what individuals and employers expected, also contained details about performance in terms of patient care. This chapter summarises and discusses performance drawing on data from all these sources and referring back to Chapters 7 and 8 (which describe individual expectations) as necessary.

WHAT WERE THE FINDINGS?

We firstly consider performance at the individual level – both how it was defined and influenced. Organisational and NHS performance is then discussed, in terms of both process and outcome, followed by explorations of the links between individual and organisational performance.

PERFORMANCE IN THE NHS – INDIVIDUALS AND ORGANISATIONS

Individual performance means providing good technical care

For most individuals, performing as an individual was about playing one's part in the provision of care – ie the process – rather than about directly influencing outcomes, although the link was recognised.

For clinical staff, the core of their work is about the technical quality of the process of care:

> Clearly, it's about performing the daily tasks, seeing the patients, doing my clinics – obviously, to a good standard ...

> (Doctor)

However, there was some concern about whether performance was assessed in this way, with a tendency to measure activity rather than impact or effectiveness raised in descriptions of individual performance:

> It is all task-orientated on me. Rather than 'Well done. That patient got well really quickly and is now back at home with his family', it's about 'The paperwork wasn't in order. That job wasn't done. That meeting wasn't attended' ... so it is all about measuring my activity rather than my effectiveness.

> (Nurse, pay band 6)

This conflict between performance measures and patient care is also reflected in descriptions of organisational performance (see section below).

Individual performance means providing good interpersonal care ...

Many staff also emphasised the interpersonal aspects of providing care. Staff (not only clinical) felt that performance was doing their bit and behaving in a certain way:

> It's actually also about behaving in the way that you are supposed to do – performing in terms of behaviour. It's really about anything you do. You do it in the best and most appropriate way that you can.

> (Director)

> Performance is how you actually do your job, how you perform it, how you actually deliver care.

> (Nurse, pay band 6)

This emphasis on the interpersonal aspect of care is also shown by responses to the question about what constitutes individual performance, for which 23% of individuals described individual performance as being about 'staff attitude and approach', focusing most commonly on 'doing my best':

> I think, generally, I do my best – and I always get positive feedback from people, so, hopefully I'm doing what's wanted from me.

> (Therapist, pay band 6)

Individual performance is 'doing what is expected'

By far the most common category of description of individual performance was 'doing what is expected' (see Table 17 on page 85). This category spanned both professional groups and levels of the organisation.

> If I was performing well, I would say I was delivering and exceeding against all expectations of me.

> (Director)

> Meeting my job description ... being an effective practitioner.

> (Nurse, pay band 3)

This was described by directors as an important factor in effective people management:

> People need to know what they are supposed to do, how they are doing, and how to put it right if they are not doing it in the right way ... We have a responsibility to staff to be clear about what's wanted.

> (Director)

Individuals also believe that their employer expects them to do the job: 62% of descriptions of what employers expected were concerned with getting the job done (functional commitment) (see Chapter 8).

Individual performance is therefore about being seen to be doing what is expected, performing well in terms of *what* you do and *how* you do it.

Influences on individual performance

Preceding chapters in this report have considered a number of areas which may influence individual performance. In this section we consider whether there is evidence from this research to show *how* these areas influence individual performance and whether there are additional factors perceived to influence individual performance not already highlighted.

The employer

In general, the evidence from the staff in contractor/partner organisations (Chapter 4) was that their performance in terms of providing patient care was often not affected by the organisation by which they were employed. Although this was not a major focus of the interviews we conducted, we found no substantial evidence to suggest that patient care was disrupted, largely because contract staff tended to retain or assume a commitment to patient care as a priority.

IS THIS SUPPORTED BY OTHER RESEARCH?

Literature on the professions highlights a difference between the ideology of administrative and professional work – ie the sets of ideas by which individuals explain and justify the ends and means (Bunderson, 2001). It is argued that professionals employed by an organisation interact with the organisation both as professionals and employees, and that as professionals they hold a predominantly relational psychological contract (see Chapter 7), but as employees the contract is predominantly transactional. If the provision of patient care is seen as part of the individual's role as a 'professional', it may be relatively unaffected by a change in employer – which would influence primarily the transactional element of the psychological contract.

HR practices

The role of HR practices in influencing individual performance was clear from various elements of the research:

❖ expectations around training

When having expectations met in terms of HR practices was mentioned, training was the most frequently mentioned HR practice (40% of all HR expectations mentioned).

Because I know I've been trained in my job, I feel that I can do it to the best of my ability.

(Clerical, pay band 2)

It improves patient care the more knowledgeable you are.

(Therapist, pay band 4)

❖ perceptions of appraisal, training and development

The role of training was also clear from individual perceptions of HR practices (Chapter 5). Performance is seen to be dependent upon the quality of skills and knowledge of individuals, and this requires appropriate appraisal, training and development.

Q: **What happened?**
A: *I was at a workforce development conference, where my expectation was that I was going to learn something.*

Q: **How did it make you feel?**
A: *I did learn something. I go to a lot of conferences where I don't learn anything. It was nice and it was refreshing to actually come out and think 'There is some knowledge that I didn't have*

before and I have got now,' and it applies to something that I want to take forward within the organisation.

Q: **What was the impact on your performance?**
A: *It will certainly help me achieve Trust objectives and be good from my performance point of view, but I think I have got a service-user focus anyway. I started life as a clinician. It sort of satisfies that part of me as a person too.*

Q: **How did it affect patient care?**
A: *It is good for our service users because that is where our objectives lead us.*

(Administrative, pay band 5)

Help and encouragement

The effect of help and encouragement in terms of expectations being met was not perceived as having a direct effect on individual performance. However, it had a clear effect on the emotional state of individuals which did in turn influence individual performance.

I think if I am feeling supported, I am probably more able to support the staff below me. I think in terms of my clinical work, I think I work in a professional way whatever is going on... but you wouldn't stay on that little bit extra, or maybe go to that meeting that was happening after work, or whatever.

(Nurse, pay band 6)

Descriptions of what encouraged extra effort also showed that the support of colleagues or managers was an influential factor, 20% of responses giving such examples.

IS THIS SUPPORTED BY OTHER RESEARCH?

The distinction between the professional and administrative ideology of work (Bunderson, 2001) is again relevant here. Provision of support to carry out the task would be viewed as an aspect of the transactional psychological contract (ie the administrative element), and therefore lack of support does not affect the professional element.

Infrastructure

In common with the accounts of having expectations met, some of the examples of the impact of infrastructure on individual performance were concerned with having enough staff, and this could be seen then to impact on patient care. However, analysis later in this chapter shows that some individuals were clear that resources were limited and that a key element of performance at both individual and organisational level is effective utilisation of resources – doing the best with what is available.

Enabling patient care

When individuals were asked about the impact of both positive and negative incidents on their personal performance, a common response was that they perceived there to be no impact on performance because they always did their best anyway. Non-clinical staff addressed this issue:

My performance stays the same – I like to think I'm professional.

(Administrative, pay band 2)

You try to work to the optimum level at all times ... I just carried on as usual.

(Hotel and estates, pay band 5)

Clinical staff also described this, showing that in this research there was no support for the view that it is only clinical professionals who do their best for the patient whatever.

We're in a caring profession, so you really shouldn't let [a negative incident] affect your performance.

(Nurse, pay band 7)

...You just get on with your job. At the end of the day you do what is right for the patient, and if that makes things slightly inconvenient for you, then that is tough.

(Doctor)

Obviously, you would never do anything detrimental for patient care. Patients are people, aren't they?

(Nurse, pay band 5)

The impact of this professional ideology of work (Bunderson, 2001) was also apparent when individuals described what influenced them to go beyond expectations, 11% of responses specifically mentioning the patient (see Chapter 8). It is also supported by the ranking by individuals in order of importance to them [1 = most important, 5 = least important] of the NHS, their Trust, the profession, their team and the patient. In general, patients were the most important and the NHS the least (see Table 15 below) although there were some small variations between case study organisations.

Emotional responses

On average, over 70% of those responding (129 replies were documented) had experienced a positive emotion as a result of having their expectations met. Typical emotional responses and the way they influence individual performance are illustrated in Table 16 (opposite) which shows high and low levels of positive and negative emotions (using a classification adapted from Watson *et al*, 1988).

However, the view that if staff are happy, they will perform better is also supported by other data. A Director described the ideal organisation as one in which staff 'feel happy and are delivering good patient care'. Other examples include:

Happy staff lead to good services and patient care.

(Director)

Table 15 ❖ Ranking of patient, team, profession, Trust and NHS

	OVERALL RANKING	Case 1	Case 2	Case 3	Case 4	Case 5	Case 6
Patient	1	1	1	1	1	1	1
Team	2	2	2	2	2	2	2
Profession	3	3	4	3	4	3	4
Trust	4	5	3	4	3	4	3
NHS	5	4	5	5	5	5	5

Table 16 ❖ Positive and negative emotions		
	Positive	**Negative**
HIGH	eg enjoying, happy	eg frustrated, irritated
	A joyful nurse is a happy patient. (Nurse, pay band 4) If someone is happy in what they are doing, they are hopefully going to be motivated to do better for the patients. We are all here to provide the best patient care. One of the ways of doing that is actually ensuring you've got a happy workforce. (Director)	If you're not very happy, then it does get reflected down to the patients and to their relatives. (Nurse, pay band 7) If I am feeling irritated and can't wait to get out of here, then on the stroke of 2.30 I am gone. (Nurse, pay band 6)
LOW	eg comfortable, OK	eg disappointed, let down
	[How you feel] affects how you are when you're seeing patients because you are relaxed and not worried about other things. You might not think it's having a positive effect, but it is. (Nurse, pay band 8)	[My expectations have not been met:] I expected professional development ... a supportive working environment ... Feeling undervalued can have a de-motivating effect ... I know that if I am working with someone who I knows values me and listens to me, then I am more motivated in terms of coming to work and doing my job. (Nurse, pay band 8)

This individual believed that sickness absence rates were a 'good indicator of how happy people are' and gave an example of a time during a merger period when rates rose significantly.

Negative emotions did not automatically have a detrimental effect on individual performance. There were a number of examples where the professional ideology of work (Bunderson, 2001) focusing on patient care was perceived to be more important than how an individual felt:

> Whatever situation I am in – whether I am stressed, whether I am upset or anything like that – I will do the work to the best of my ability. I will never let anything affect my work. I try not to. I like to think it doesn't, anyway.
>
> (Administrative, pay band 4)

> It didn't change my performance [referring to a negative incident at work] ... What needed to be done was done. It was just that little bit harder to be smiling because inside I didn't know if I wanted to.
>
> (Manager, pay band 7)

> I felt very hurt and very demoralised – but I would like to think it didn't affect my performance in doing my job or thinking 'Why am I here?'
>
> (Administrative, pay band 4)

> I felt devalued – I wouldn't recommend my friends or family to work for the NHS ... I maintain a certain level of professionalism but don't do any more than asked because there is no incentive to do so.
>
> (Scientist, pay band 6)

Feedback on individual performance

Individual performance was in some cases described as being influenced by emotion after previous performance was recognised, because it gave rise to positive emotions. Recognition of performance could be in terms of formally recognised achievement:

> The feeling is good ... It makes you perform better. It increases your performance. The more achievement you get, the more achievement you want in that area.
>
> (Scientist, pay band 7)

If anyone feels they are actually achieving their goals, obviously they perform better, don't they?

(Administrative, pay band 8)

However, formal feedback systems may not always give the information that is helpful:

I think that the kinds of targets that have been identified don't really reflect what I think is valuable about performance ... We use a system which is hopeless at giving us back the information that we want to have. I and my colleagues would like to be able to use the figures that we give in ... We did contribute to that.

(Therapist, pay band 8)

However, the sense of 'making a difference' was also important to some individuals, rather than formal measurement of performance:

If things are going well and you are thinking, 'Yes, I can make a difference,' it makes you happy within yourself. It gives you more confidence to come to work every day and think, 'Yes, I'm doing the right thing.' It gives you a lot of good feedback for yourself.

(Nurse, pay band 5)

If you think people are appreciating you and are thinking you can do your job, you do your job better.

(Administrative, pay band 2)

Q: **What happened?**
A: *The PCT introduced 'listeners' who weren't managers, who staff can approach when they are concerned about bullying and harassment. I volunteered for that. I've had one phonecall.*

Q: **How did it make you feel?**
A: *You become aware that people are under stress There is a fine line between too much work and feeling it as harassment. It has made me more aware of people's different reactions to the same level of work or home pressures.*

Q: *How did it affect patient care?*
A: *If somebody feels threatened, they don't work to an optimal level – they may go off sick. How people answer the phones to patients also affects patient care.*

(Support worker, pay band 4)

Appreciation from patients or relatives was particularly highlighted as encouraging:

Sometimes you are rushing around and it can get you down, but if somebody says, 'Oh, thank you. You have really helped me – I was frightened,' it sort of makes you feel positive about why you are doing it. It gives you a feeling that it is not just 'how many you can get on the scanner' but it is what you do as you are doing your job that is important.

(Therapist, pay band 6)

I have got newspapers which I take onto one of the wards ... When I go on there, I will take them to the patients and I will talk to any of them, and they look forward to talking to me. When you walk away and you hear them say, 'She's a nice girl,' it encourages you to do the same thing again tomorrow.

(Support worker, pay band 2)

Q: **What happened?**
A: We've had quite a difficult patient with difficult relatives. We were a bit wary of their expectations of what we could offer for the patient. But on discharge they did actually thank us and said that they felt he wouldn't have got the care that he received here anywhere else.

Q: **How did it make you feel?**
A: We were all being a bit negative about it, but it came out quite positive, really.

Q: **What was the impact on your performance?**
A: We do give good patient care and I think we just carried on and tried to make it – we always aim for 100%.

Q: **How did it affect patient care?**
A: The patient got a good standard of care.

(Clinical manager, pay band 7)

Directors also highlighted the importance of feedback for improving performance:

> *Encouraging and developing people (the carrot) works ... seeing that what you do makes a difference to patient care. A negative approach (the stick) doesn't.*

(Director)

Q: **What happened?**
A: *We stepped up a gear because of strikes at the ambulance and fire service. It was recognised. We always get a nice letter from our director of service provision to say that she appreciates what the team has done.*

Q: **How did it make you feel?**
A: *It boosts morale. We feel people are proud of our service, and if people come to visit the Trust, it's one of the places that they like to bring people.*

Q: **What was the impact on your performance?**
A: *It affects how you are when you're seeing patients because you are relaxed and not worried about other things. You might not think it's having a positive effect – but it is.*

Q: **How did it affect patient care?**
A: *The majority of our patients go away and they have a good experience of the NHS.*

(Nurse, pay band 8)

Organisational performance: the process of care

In asking individuals about organisational performance we were not seeking absolute measures but a deeper understanding of what they thought organisational performance was, and the factors that influenced it. Objective measures of performance for each case are described in Chapter 3.

Targets as a measure of performance

> *Performance is measured by hitting targets or not hitting targets ... for the PCT and the NHS as a whole.*

(Support worker, pay band 4)

WHAT ARE TARGETS?

The term 'targets' was commonly used when describing organisational performance, although often without being specific about which targets were meant. Because this research was carried out after the publication of the last 'star ratings' but before the publication of the first ratings from the Healthcare Commission's Annual Health Check assessment (see Chapter 3), it has been assumed that 'targets' refer to those in the star ratings – and the vast majority of these are concerned with the process of care – so that the only 'outcome' ones are mortality measures. The Annual Health Check still incorporates almost all of the areas previously assessed: many of the 'targets' still exist.

We have therefore assumed that when the term 'targets' is used, it refers to measures of the process of care.

The emphasis on waiting times and lists in the star ratings was reflected in the responses from individuals:

> *Well, we are talking about waiting lists, really, aren't we?*

(Administrative, pay band 2)

> *'Performance' for the Trust means statistics, contracts, waiting lists, waiting times for people between being referred and getting an assessment, and then treatment waiting time.*

(Therapist, pay band 8)

The emphasis was very clearly on targets that involved activities that were being *measured*:

> *It's a mixture of targets, assessments – like our cancer waiting-time target – standards for MRSA, A&E targets, how many patients are seen within four hours, etc. Also, in terms of finance, how we are performing – are we in budget, out of budget?*

(Administrative, pay band 8)

> *Standards of staff working, standards of service ... monitoring performance, clinical governance issues – it's about achieving things that are measurable standards.*

(Therapist, pay band 6)

But it is also about the interpersonal aspects of care...

Just as individual performance was described as being about *how* you do your job, there was also some recognition that organisational performance in terms of process might be a mixture of things – not always just 'targets' which appear to measure technical quality of care. The interpersonal aspects of care were also important – and it is these that were often referred to as 'patient care'. Some individuals felt that both aspects were part of the whole which is 'performance'.

> *'Performance' means how you operate, the sort of service you provide, the treatment people get, the waiting times – everything.*
>
> (Support worker, pay band 2)

Targets and interpersonal care are conflicting

Some individuals saw a potential conflict between technical care and interpersonal care – 'patient care' thus conflicting with meeting targets – although this conflict was not highlighted by either the majority of individuals or predominantly by clinical staff:

> *'Performance' in the NHS is a two-part thing. The two parts don't fit together. There aren't many people in the NHS that are interested in both parts. One part is about quality of care and medical outcome, and one part is about running the business – and they don't sit comfortably together. Dependent on who you are talking to, and the time of the month in terms of what pressures are on the business, and the time of the year, one or other of the performance conversations will happen.*
>
> (HR professional, pay band 8)

> *If I was talking 'performance' from a clinical area, I would be looking at high-quality care on the nursing side. On the managers' part I would be looking at achieving targets.*
>
> (HR professional, pay band 4)

There was, however, a vocal minority with strong views expressed:

> *We are all supposed to be here for the good of patients, but sadly, you do hear quoted on quite a few occasions in recent times, 'God forbid we should ever do anything for the benefit of patients.' It seems that performance is all about getting figures and meeting targets and stuff like that, and sometimes I think the patient gets overlooked.*
>
> (Support worker, pay band 4)

> *I think sometimes the hospitals are focusing more on getting the stars than making sure the patient gets what they need.*
>
> (Support worker, pay band 4)

> *You'd like to think performance was about patient care and doing the best for patients, but I'm not sure now whether it isn't bums on beds and saving money.*
>
> (Therapist, pay band 7)

Some clinical staff did, however, feel that their own professional standards were in conflict with the national performance requirements:

> *There are professional standards for public health specialists, peer standards, personal standards (why I'm here, why I'm doing it) which don't necessarily fit with any of the above [targets] ...*
>
> (Doctor)

> *I think the definition of 'performance' depends on who you talk to in the Trust, on which part of the Trust they work in. I feel that for a clinician like me, performance is very face-to-face patient care.*
>
> (Therapist, pay band 8)

Some people mentioned that they felt they were trying to deliver patient care *despite* targets, or recognised the challenges in balancing the two.

> *I think it's about hitting the targets and satisfying our political masters, but actually it's about doing the right thing for the local population and our patients in spite of all of that.*
>
> (Director)

> *I think it's just important to reach targets while not impacting on patient care ... just making sure they're hand-in-hand and one's not going over the other.*
>
> (Administrative, pay band 5)

> *We have this saying that 'performance isn't about meeting targets'. It's the whole atmosphere of the place as well – the character of the place – as to whether the patient gets a good experience or not. It's whether patients go, saying 'That was a fantastic experience!' If they can go out saying that, we've performed well.*
>
> (Therapist, pay band 8)

IS THIS SUPPORTED BY OTHER RESEARCH?

Contrary to our findings there is a view that 'clinical staff may be more concerned with measures of medical outcomes (eg re-infection rates) and administrative staff with measures of outputs (eg number of patients handled)' (Ballantine *et al*, 1998; p.72).

Levels of performance – the common themes

The main categories of response to the question 'What is performance?' for the NHS, organisation and individual are shown in Table 17 below. Only the major categories (with more than 10% of responses) are shown. There are various insights demonstrated by this data.

Are NHS and organisational performance perceived as the same thing?

Answers to this varied. Some described organisational performance as 'the same as for the NHS, I suppose', but there were others who made a differentiation or were more specific about how their general responses about NHS performance were interpreted locally within the organisation, which gave some helpful insights into perceptions of performance.

Although the NHS is seen as providing patient care, this is emphasised more in terms of the local organisation. The prevailing view of NHS performance is that it is about 'targets', although patient care and outcomes also feature:

From a performance point of view, I suppose, the top line is really that the NHS is ... helping the patients. They're there to help the patients maintain good health as well as actually promote good health in people.

(Administrative, pay band 3)

The focus on external results – reputation, etc – in terms of organisation performance was not something that might have been expected, and was not related to the status of the organisations, although two were already Foundation Trusts.

Does the local population have confidence in the hospital? Are people happy to come here? The Trust performance is gauged by what the local people have to say when you are out and about ... You overhear conversations when you're in pubs – you hear that people have to go to the hospital and it's not that bad.

(Radiologist, pay band 6)

The corporate view of performance would be that it's managed to get Foundation status. If the government has thought fit to give our Trust Foundation status, then it must be performing well, according to the government. I've certainly got no better indicator of how a body is, or how an organisation is performing.

(Doctor)

Table 17 ❖ Common performance themes			
	NHS performance (as % of total responses n=106)	Organisational performance (as % of total responses n=90)	Individual performance (as % of total responses n=107)
'Targets'	23	24	Not mentioned
'Targets' and patient care	28	4	Not mentioned
Patient care/meeting patient needs	15	32	12
Utilisation of resources	10	8	8
Reputation with others (patients/staff/community)	Not mentioned	16	Not mentioned
Doing what is expected in the role	Not mentioned	Not mentioned	47
Staff attitude and approach	Not mentioned	Not mentioned	23
Being competent to do the job	Not mentioned	Not mentioned	10

PERFORMANCE IN THE NHS – INDIVIDUALS AND ORGANISATIONS

85

LIVERPOOL JOHN MOORES UNIVERSITY
LEARNING SERVICES

Table 18 ❖ Performance as patient care	
NHS	*I think it involves patient care and waiting lists and just making the service better for patients.* (Administrative, pay band 3)
Organisation	*Performance of the trust can be linked into patient care which can be linked into resources ... financial, human resources – but it all boils down to the most important thing, which is patient care.* (Nurse, pay band 5)
Individual	*I just want to provide a really good service for current service users ... At the end of the day, if a service user needs a service and I am coming to the end of my budget, I will say 'Bugger the budget,' and still provide the service – and get into trouble for it.* (Therapist, pay band 7)

Is organisational performance about the process of care or the outcomes of care?

There was recognition that both process and outcome contribute to the overall 'performance' of the organisation.

> *I think you can look at performance in terms of effective treatment for illness or injury. So that is obviously measured by how long people stay in hospital, how long it takes them to get into hospital, what the waiting times are. If you look at things like surgery, the success rate or death rate of individual surgeons – they are all performance indicators.*

> (Nurse, pay band 6)

However, there was a view that there was not sufficient measurement of outcomes – and this was especially seen in responses from mental health organisations, from both clinical and administrative staff:

> *In the NHS the input tends to get managed, which really isn't valuable. Outputs sometimes get measured. But certainly from a performance point of view, I think it's important in all areas to look at the process side to make sure that whatever the output is, the process of getting it is the most effective.*

> (Manager, pay band 8)

> *I think working in mental health the indicators about effective treatment are much harder to judge. And I think in this organisation they tend to manage/ monitor performance more by staff activity than by patient outcomes.*

> (Nurse, pay band 6)

In general, there was relatively little focus on outcomes when individuals were asked to describe performance.

> ### IS THIS SUPPORTED BY OTHER RESEARCH?
>
> Because outcomes may be viewed as a consequence of the process of care (Campbell *et al*, 2000) it is perhaps not surprising that outcomes were not commonly mentioned by those who are directly involved in the process when asked about their views on performance. However, this might also demonstrate a lack of understanding of how the process of care impacts on outcomes.

What are the common features of individual and organisational performance?

The two common themes were 'patient care' and use of resources, which were also mentioned at the level of the NHS (see Table 17 on page 85).

Examples of these are given in Table 18 above.

Some staff could clearly describe the link between what they did as individuals and the process of providing patient care, even though they were not directly involved themselves in providing patient care:

> *Whatever we do affects patient care. We're setting a rota for our patient-trackers to track the patients. That wouldn't appear to have an input into patient care directly – but indirectly it does. If the patient-trackers don't work to the best of their ability (they are trained and competent in their roles), then a patient will slip through the net and they will possibly breach a target – which would have an impact on the Trust in the terms of star rating, etc.*

> (Clinical manager, pay band 8)

Staff from the HR function differed in their descriptions of the impact of their work on patient care:

> *Performance is about seeing the outcomes of what we do ... You can actually see something making a difference, having a benefit for the end user. Although I'm not directly involved with patient care, I support the staff that are, so I would expect them to see a benefit [from what I do], and hopefully that would then impact on the care that they are able to provide.*
>
> (HR professional, pay band 8)

> *In terms of patient care it is very hard for a human resources department, and certainly a training department, to say 'By me teaching X, the patient Joe Bloggs who comes through A&E next week is going to be treated in a different way.' ... I think there are too many variables for me to say 'Yes, X attended this and the outcome for that patient was that.'*
>
> (HR training professional, pay band 8)

Q: **What happened?**
A: *I'm an HR manager and spent hours with a distressed member of staff who was [through Agenda for Change] put on a lower band than she expected. I managed to get a better grade for her. She just emailed to say 'Thank you'.*

Q: **How did it make you feel?**
A: *I was quite pleased. It felt nice that someone bothered to say 'thank you'.*

Q: **What was the impact on your performance?**
A: *It reinforced what I would do ... Try to meet people's needs.*

Q: **How did it affect patient care?**
A: *The member of staff didn't leave, and now she will be able to concentrate on her job. She was having sleepless nights, but now she's no longer distracted, and that will have a positive impact on her work and the team she manages.*

(HR professional, pay band 8)

Utilisation of resources and/or value for money was the other common theme which, although not mentioned by a large proportion of individuals, demonstrates that the reality of a resource-limited environment is recognised by some within organisations. This was especially clear when a description of individual performance was given in relation to positive or negative experiences at work. In examples of working beyond expectations there was also often reference to use of resources – being more efficient in doing the work, or freeing up more time to get things done. Examples are shown in Table 19 below.

Levels of performance – how they are linked

There were a variety of insights into the mechanism by which these levels are linked.

No clear links

There were individuals who were clear that 'targets' did not relate to their own individual performance but were something at an organisational level – individual performance was much more about the process of care, and individual motivation and ability.

> *Individual performance is the ability of an individual to carry out their assigned tasks in a competent way. Performance for the department moves on to more*

Table 19 ❖	Performance as use of resources
NHS	*Performance is providing a high standard of service within the given resource.* (Nurse, pay band 8) *Providing good-quality services at reasonable cost to the taxpayer.* (Therapist, pay band 7)
Organisation	*The most you can to the benefit of the patient with the resources that you have.* (Pharmacist, pay band 8) *Using the resources that we've got efficiently and effectively, whether it is the staff or the finance that we've got.* (HR professional, pay band 7)
Individual	*That I'm doing the best I can with the time and resources that we've got.* (Therapist, pay band 7)

target-driven things and patient numbers, unit costs for various training, etc.

(Radiologist, pay band 6)

My performance, personally, is how I treat people and how I deal with situations and what I can do for people. But I'm very conscious that performance at the PCT level is about ... reaching their targets which are set by the NHS.

(Nurse, pay band 6)

They therefore found it difficult to link their individual performance to that of the organisation, and showed that for them individual performance was about *how* care was provided (interpersonal), whereas organisational performance was about 'targets' (technical). If individuals cannot clearly see a link between organisational objectives and what they do, they are unlikely to prioritise the achievement of organisational objectives.

This ambivalence about the link between the individual and organisation is also shown by the analysis of ratings of statements:

Statement:	1 strongly agree 2 agree 3 not sure 4 disagree 5 strongly disagree	ANOVA (p<.05, two-tailed)
I really feel as if the Trust's problems are my own	mean score: 2.82 [not sure]	❖ No significant links

Organisational and individual performance: a downwards or upwards link?

A number of individuals suggested that individual objectives and performance were in some way cascaded down from organisational objectives, whereas others saw individual performance as making an upwards contribution to organisational and NHS performance. The upwards link was mentioned more often – which is to be expected, since individuals were being asked about their perspective, so it is likely that they would start from there (see Table 20 below).

Some staff who had been part of a process of job specification using the Knowledge and Skills Framework – a national competency framework for the NHS – felt that this showed the upwards link clearly:

Now with the KSF and the PDPs it's all linked, because you've got a business plan which is basically dictated from government, which the [Trust] has, and you work out your KSF and you work out your levels on what you say you are going to do. This has to be reflected by the business plan and ultimately the government target. So your performance basically is just a straight line up.

(Nurse, pay band 6)

I'm expected to do things to do with the KSF and to meet the criteria, really. So your own bit of performance is measured against those KSF competencies, and then targets really for the [Trust] and the NHS generally.

(Administrative, pay band 4)

Table 20 ❖ **Upwards and downwards links between individual and organisational performance**

Linking from the top down	Linking upwards
It's the same measures [as for the NHS] but just doing it at a local level and then dividing it down even further to clinical team level. (Administrative, pay band 8)	*I mean, obviously you've got your objectives and stuff on a team level, and then higher up within the NHS, sort of Department of Health guidelines on performance, etc.* (Therapist, pay band 7) *I talk about the Trust performing well – I don't talk about myself performing well. It's a corporate entity. Performance of the Trust is determined by the contribution of everyone.* (Director) *Performance depends on whether you are looking at personal performance or the Trust's targeted performance. Personal performance would be about ensuring that somebody has got the competence to do the job, is happy, has got the work–life balance, [has] got a personal development plan that meets their needs but also meets the Trust's needs ... Trust performance is a lot around target-driven performance.* (Radiologist, pay band 8)

CONCLUSIONS

Individual performance is about involvement in the process of providing healthcare ('patient care'), which then leads to outcomes for patients and is considered to be not just about what an individual does (the technical element of providing healthcare) but also about how it is done (the interpersonal element). Targets for performance are seen to be important at the organisational level but much less so at an individual level, where the focus is on the interpersonal aspects of providing healthcare. Individual performance is perceived to be influenced by a variety of factors, including the organisation that employs the individual, HR practices – specifically training and development – help and encouragement from colleagues and managers, the organisational infrastructure – specifically the level of staffing, the professional ideology of staff, individual emotions arising from having expectations met and feedback on performance – both formal measurement and informal encouragement.

Organisational performance is concerned with both the process of care and the outcome of care, targets being concerned with the process of care (the technical element) and the aspects of that which can be measured. Although some staff felt that patient care (interpersonal) and targets were in conflict, they were not a majority of individuals, nor were they only clinical staff that highlighted this.

Patient care and the use of resources are the two elements of performance that were common to NHS, organisational and individual performance. Some individuals saw no link between individual and organisational performance, but many did, and expressed it both as organisational objectives being broken down into individual ones, and as individual performances combining to achieve organisational performance.

What are the links with the rest of the research?

❖ Individual performance is influenced by the individuals themselves – their professional ideology and their emotions.

❖ Individual performance is influenced by infrastructure, help and encouragement from others and feedback on performance.

❖ Individual performance is influenced by training (HRM content).

❖ Some individuals saw no link between individual and organisational performance, but many did, and expressed this both as organisational objectives being broken down into individual ones, and as individual performances combining to achieve organisational performance.

❖ Organisational performance is linked to organisational strategy, which in turn is dependent on the wider context of national performance measurement requirements – especially those concerned with 'targets'.

LEARNING POINTS

❖ Both individual and organisational performance is concerned with the process of providing healthcare – *how* this is done – rather than the outcomes of the process.

❖ Individuals do not often make the link between what they do and the measures used to assess organisational performance – specifically those described as 'targets'.

❖ Emotional response is part of a process whereby an incident invokes a reaction which then affects behaviour and performance.

For the organisation as a whole

Organisations must support individuals to develop *how* healthcare is provided.
A focus on outcomes without considering the process by which outcomes are achieved may not be an effective use of resources.

Alignment between the values of the organisation, its vision and objectives, and the role of the individual helps the individual to understand how his or her work fits with the organisation as a whole. This alignment has to be made explicit and communicated clearly from the top.

Organisations must recognise that emotional response is a part of the process leading to individual performance – and may require support.

PERFORMANCE IN THE NHS – INDIVIDUALS AND ORGANISATIONS

❖ Negative emotion does not automatically lead to poor individual performance, due to the professional ideology of NHS staff.

> Organisations must develop appropriate strategies to support individuals who experience negative emotions, even if the individuals do not allow this to impact on patient care.

❖ Communication to individuals about performance – both from formal assessment systems and from informal recognition – makes a difference to individual performance.

> Organisations must ensure both that such communication is provided through effective and timely mechanisms and that the feedback is meaningful. IT may be able to support this process.

❖ Individuals do have concerns about the reputation of the organisation they work for, both locally and nationally, in terms of performance.

> There must be a greater understanding of the importance of organisational reputation and the impact this has on staff who work for the organisation or its partners.

❖ Help and encouragement is an influence on individual performance.

> Enabling and encouraging a supportive workplace for all staff should be a priority for the organisation – because it influences performance – and is not simply the responsibility of the HR function.

For the HRM system and the HR function

❖ HR practices – particularly training – have an influence on individual performance.

> HR has to ensure that practices are adapted as appropriate to the needs of the individual, especially where training is concerned.

> HR can support the development of this understanding by aligning individual and organisational performance through competency frameworks which link these levels clearly.

❖ Individuals do not often make the link between what they do and the measures used to assess organisational performance – specifically those described as 'targets'.

> HR can support managers to explain how 'targets' can be linked to the role of the individual and to a focus on the patient.

❖ Some individuals can clearly see the links between what they do and patient care, even where they are not directly involved in the patient care process.

> Organisations must ensure that individuals understand how what they do is aligned with patient care. This is likely to require detailed understanding of *how* work links to patients, not simply a series of statements about patient care being the priority.

CONCLUSIONS

INTRODUCTION

For a brief summary of research findings, see also Boaden *et al* (2007).

This report has presented and analysed data from empirical research at six NHS case study organisations which gives insight into the question

> *How can HRM help NHS organisations achieve their goals?*

It concludes that HRM can help by:

❖ identifying the process by which HRM helps organisations to achieve their goals

❖ engaging with the various parts of the process, especially the individuals in the organisation and any partner organisations

❖ aligning elements of the process, especially the links between organisational strategy and individual roles.

At all stages, the enablers of engagement and alignment, as well as the constraints, have to be identified and managed appropriately. This is not a role solely for the HR function although HR can lead on ensuring that processes are enabled effectively. Our findings suggest that there is no one 'best way' for HRM to operate in NHS organisations. Instead, HRM systems must become increasingly sophisticated in engaging with a range of stakeholders to enable improvements in performance.

This chapter summarises the key conclusions from each of these elements of the framework. It also describes the links

between these elements which constitute the process of HRM engagement and alignment as part of the overall process of linking HRM to performance.

KEY CONCLUSIONS

The framework developed to analyse the data is shown in Figure 11 on page 92 (and has featured throughout the report).

The conclusions from each part of the research are summarised in the sections below.

Organisation strategy and structure

❖ Each organisation had developed its own organisational strategies in response to the wider context and local circumstances. There was little commonality in terms of organisational strategy content between the various types of organisation – eg Acute Trusts. National performance data was not sensitive enough to indicate some of this variety, however.

HRM systems

❖ There was some divergence in terms of HRM strategy or structure in the case study organisations, again reflecting a variety of responses to the wider context.

❖ HRM strategy in terms of cross-organisational contracting varied across organisations and was affected by the types of arrangements and structures put in place to manage relationships, its ambiguity and complexity increased by

Figure 11 ❖ **A framework for analysis**

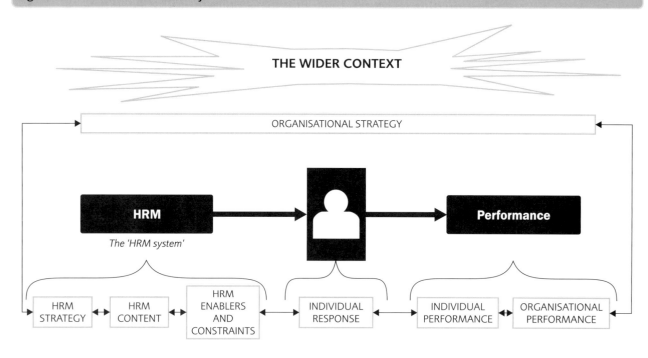

fragmented relationships and differences in pay, terms and conditions. However, even if people working for contractors or partners did not feel particularly enamoured by their employer's HR practices, they tended to minimise any negative impact on patient care.

❖ Although HRM content (practices) was similar in each case study organisation, the priority given to different practices by the leaders of the organisation varied and was often a reflection of the organisational strategy.

❖ HRM content can be brought to life by the work of line managers who recognise the importance of HRM. Line managers had little engagement with the development of HR policies however, and HRM was given low priority in comparison to other activities.

❖ Individual perceptions of HR practices (content) tended to group them into those that support *professional development* through appraisal, training and career development, those that rely on *employee contribution* through communication, teamworking and employee involvement. and those that correspond to *the employee 'deal'* involving recruitment, pay, non-monetary rewards, work–life balance and job security.

The individual

We focused here on the psychological contract as a framework for analysis of individual perceptions.

❖ Expectations at work can be both explicit (ie openly discussed) and tacit (ie taken for granted or not openly discussed) and classified into one of four types: HR practices, help and encouragement, infrastructure, and enabling patient care.

❖ We found elements of ideological, relational and transactional issues within the psychological contracts of NHS employees and organisations.

❖ Over 70% of individuals had their expectations met at work, and many felt that there was a connection between met expectations and delivery of patient care.

❖ Most individuals thought that their employers expected them to get the job done (task performance), which may reflect a professional ideology that implies that getting the job done contributes to patient care.

❖ Going beyond employer expectations (contextual performance) was most commonly described in terms of staying later at work than planned or expected, and was generally perceived as being linked to patient care.

Performance

❖ Individual performance was perceived to be concerned with involvement in the process of providing healthcare ('patient care'), which then leads to outcomes for patients – it is about *how* an individual does his or her work.

❖ Organisational performance was assessed using 'targets' for aspects of the process of care, which were seen by some (but not the majority) to be in conflict with patient care.

❖ Patient care and the use of resources were the two elements of performance described common to NHS, organisational and individual performance.

❖ The link between individual and organisational performance was not commonly made by individuals, but where it was, individual performance was seen to contribute upwards to organisational performance.

IMPLICATIONS FOR THE NHS

We can now show *how* HRM can influence performance by presenting the implications of this research for NHS organisations and the HR function under the elements of our framework. For ease of reference, the chapter of this Report that contains the details of the conclusions and implications described is listed against each of them. Moreover, a number of these implications are supported by a recent report on the state of NHS leadership and management (NHS Confederation, 2007b), key points from which are also listed where relevant.

The implications for organisations and the HR function can be summarised in terms of three activities:

❖ Identify the stages of the *process* by which HRM helps organisations to achieve their goals, focusing specifically on the part individuals play in this. There will also be specific roles for the HR function.

❖ *Align* elements of the process, especially the links between organisational strategy and individual roles.

❖ Enable HRM to *engage* with various parts of the process by:

   ❖ *translating and adapting* policy into local actions, as well as flexibility in terms of the implementation of HR practices and policies

   ❖ *communicating* in terms of both internal and external communication, using formal and informal communication mechanisms

   ❖ *understanding*, with a focus on developing a deeper understanding of the individuals who provide healthcare, including the organisation's workforce as well as those employed by other agencies.

It is recognised that the organisation as a whole and the HR function must work closely together on many of these implications, but the distinction made here is intended to emphasise where the primary responsibility for driving these implications lies.

Figure 12 ❖ The processes linking HRM and performance

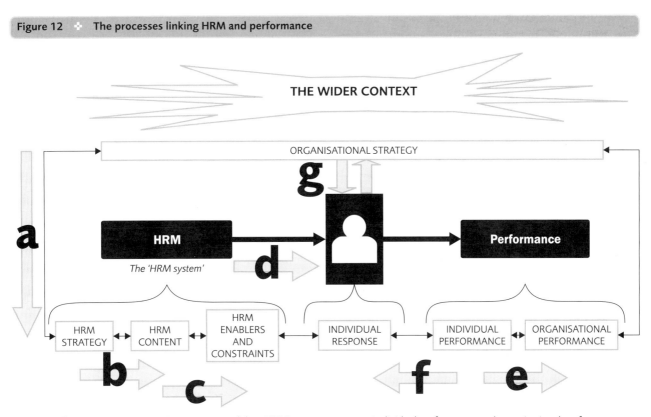

a   The wider context to organisation strategy and then HRM strategy
b   The HRM system: HRM strategy and HRM content
c   The HRM system: HRM content and implementation
d   The HRM system and the individual

e   Individual performance and organisational performance
f   Feedback about individual performance and response
g   The individual and the organisation

THE PROCESS LINKING HRM AND PERFORMANCE

This process comprises a number of sub-processes which act in a single direction. However, there may also be a similar process acting in the opposite direction; these are shown where they are important. The processes are shown in Figure 12 on page 93.

a   The wider context to organisation strategy

Involvement in both developing and monitoring organisational strategy will help individuals to see the link between their role, the goals of the organisation and the wider context (Chapter 3).

The organisation must:

❖ *align* all elements of strategy with the overall direction of the organisation – including the HRM strategy. Organisations may have to create the opportunity to do this as well as exploiting opportunities that arise – eg the prospect of Foundation status.

The HR function must:

❖ *translate and adapt* national guidance on HRM and apply it locally, in line with the intention of the NHS as a whole and its direction of travel (Chapter 3).

❖ *understand* that staff at higher levels of the organisation are more able to link the appraisal of their own role to what the organisation does. Staff at lower levels therefore need to be enabled to develop this understanding (Chapter 5).

b   The HRM system: HRM strategy and HRM content

The organisation must:

❖ *align* the capacity of the HR function with the needs of the organisation, so that it can provide effective and timely support and advice for line managers on HRM as well as fulfilling its other roles (Chapter 6).

❖ *understand* the competing priorities and the managerial skills of line managers – HRM implementation is only one of their responsibilities. This understanding must then lead to effective job design; otherwise, devolution of responsibility for HRM will not be effective (Chapter 6).

Middle managers ... are often disempowered and need more support.

NHS Confederation (2007b)

The HR function must:

❖ *align* its structure with the operating units which comprise the organisation, so that links are clear, but also support these in practice by making HR staff visible and part of the formal and informal communication networks in the organisation (Chapter 3).

❖ *communicate* with a wider range and level of staff in the development of policies to support people management (Chapter 6).

When working with partner organisations, the organisation must:

❖ *align* the positive attitudes that most people working for partners and contractors have towards providing patient care with the goals and values of the NHS, whoever the employer is (Chapter 4).

❖ *align* principles and ways of working with partner organisations. Contracts should contain clauses stipulating a similar philosophy of 'good' HR practice. These should be detailed in terms of policy, practice and communication mechanisms and may involve joint monitoring by both parties (Chapter 4).

❖ set up and facilitate a series of working teams at different levels, comprising managers from the NHS and partner/contractor organisations, to *communicate* and develop positive working relationships (Chapter 4).

c   The HRM system: HRM content and implementation

The HR function must:

❖ ensure that policies, as well as the rationale for their use and guidance on implementation, are *translated and adapted* to be clear and understandable (Chapter 6).

❖ recognise that one size will not fit all, and so *translate and adapt* HR practices in the knowledge that different emphases, depending on the organisational strategy, will be required (Chapter 5).

❖ *understand* that line managers have a key role in implementing HRM – and they have to be trained and developed to ensure that they have the knowledge and skills to deal with people management issues. They also require appropriate appraisal systems for this element of their role (Chapter 6).

d   The HRM system and the individual

The organisation must:

❖ enable and encourage a working environment which is *aligned* with the needs and expectations of staff for support from managers and colleagues – because it influences performance. This is not simply the responsibility of the HR function (Chapter 7).

The HR function must:

❖ *align* the understanding of HRM as 'people management' throughout the organisation so that HRM can achieve its objectives. At present the understanding varies according to the level of the organisation (Chapter 5).

❖ *align* practices and processes to key organisational goals, so that staff are encouraged to contribute to them and there is gain for the individual and the organisation. This can be done through effective communication, teamworking and employee involvement (Chapter 5).

❖ ensure that individuals understand the requirements of the job, as well as *translating* work requirements into specific roles with realistic demands. This will then avoid detrimental effects on individuals or others in their team (Chapter 8).

The size of the workload and unrelenting pressure can stop managers from carrying out the work they should be doing.

NHS Confederation (2007b)

❖ *adapt* HR practices to the needs of the individual as flexibly as possible, especially where training is concerned (Chapters 5, 6 and 9).

Training can be inadequate, or non-existent, at all levels of management.

NHS Confederation (2007b)

❖ *communicate* clearly the long-term implications of working long hours over a sustained period, as well as supporting individuals to address the issue. Line managers are important in this process (Chapter 8).

❖ *understand* that staff want a fair and equitable 'deal' in return for their continuing contribution to patient care – through competitive pay and rewards, work–life balance and security (Chapter 5).

❖ *understand* that staff want opportunities for developing their professional skills – through focused and integrated systems for appraisal, training and career development. Training has been shown to influence individual performance.

❖ *understand* that team-work can be effective in supporting individuals when they have issues of workload, and so encourage and support it. Line managers are also important in this process (Chapter 8).

e   Individual performance and organisational performance

The organisation must:

❖ *align* the work of individuals with patient care. This is likely to require detailed understanding of *how* work links to patient care – not simply a series of statements about patient care being a priority – and it may be more important for staff who are not directly involved in providing patient care (Chapter 9).

Managers are forced to focus upwards...and not across their Trusts towards the interests of patients and staff.

NHS Confederation (2007b)

❖ *align* performance frameworks to focus on *how* healthcare is provided. A focus on outcomes without considering the process by which outcomes are achieved may not be an effective use of resources (Chapter 9).

❖ *align* the values of the organisation, its vision and objectives, and the role of the individual. This is important so that individuals understand how their work contributes to the organisation as a whole. The alignment has to be made explicit and communicated clearly from the top (Chapter 8).

What would make a difference? A clear strategy understood by all staff.

NHS Confederation (2007b)

f   Feedback about individual performance and individual response

The organisation must:

❖ Ensure that mechanisms for *communicating* feedback are effective and timely, and that the feedback is meaningful. IT may be able to support this process (Chapter 9).

g   The individual and the organisation

The implications in this section relate to the relationship of the individuals with the organisation as a whole. Although some of them relate indirectly to the role of the HR function, they ought to be implemented by the organisation as a whole for them to have the impact on performance demonstrated by this research.

The organisation must:

❖ *align* the provision of infrastructure – including staffing levels – with work/role requirements down to the individual level. A lack of alignment leads to weakened performance (Chapter 7).

> *You have to have clear goals and achievable goals – and you have to support [middle managers].*
>
> NHS Confederation (2007b)

❖ *align* the formal and informal 'messages' that are sent to individuals about what they can expect from the organisation. These often appear to be inconsistent. This will involve HRM systems, policies and procedures, as well as other management processes (Chapter 7).

❖ *communicate* the vision for the organisation effectively so that staff at all levels can understand the link between the strategy and objectives of the organisation and their own role and development (Chapter 3).

❖ be honest and keep individuals involved and informed through effective *communication* in times of organisational change. There is a role here for the HR function to support engagement with staff (Chapter 7).

❖ *communicate* clearly that although individuals do at times work beyond employer expectations in terms of time spent, it should not become something relied on by employers on a regular basis. This involves the development of an organisational culture in which it is acceptable to raise issues of workload, through effective relationships and also through HR policies such as communication and appraisal (Chapter 8).

❖ *understand* the effect that organisational reputation has on individual motivation and behaviour, for staff working for the organisation or its partners (Chapter 9).

❖ *understand* that individuals do have expectations of their employers. These expectations may concern HR practices and other aspects of the employment relationship, but others have wider implications. A uniform response should not be assumed (Chapter 7).

> *Boards must ... pay close attention to the details of their patients' and employees' everyday experience.*
>
> NHS Confederation (2007b)

❖ *understand* that staff have a professional ideology – a set of values about their work – which must be clearly understood and supported if performance is to be sustained. This is something that makes the NHS different from other types of organisation (Chapter 7).

> *The centre could ... put more emphasis on ensuring that behaviours, policies and all aspects of the system really reflect the values people believe should be part of the NHS.*
>
> NHS Confederation (2007b)

❖ *understand* that individuals believe that they are enabled to meet the expectations of their employer because of colleagues and team-work, and then promote effective team-work and provide opportunities for informal support.

❖ *understand* why and when individuals go beyond expectations both in terms of what they do and how much time they spend. If this points up underlying system issues, these should be resolved. There may be a role for the HR function in this (Chapter 8).

❖ *understand* the implications of having some senior staff who do not believe anything is beyond employer expectations. Not only could this be detrimental to their overall work–life balance, and to the organisation as a whole, it is also a poor example of working practices. The boundaries of every job should be set so they are reasonable; otherwise, there is a risk of burnout (Chapter 8).

❖ *understand* that emotional response is a part of the process leading to individual performance. Although negative emotion does not automatically lead to poor individual performance because of the professional ideology of staff, individuals may still require support from the organisation (Chapter 9).

The HR function must:

❖ *align* individual and organisational performance through competency frameworks which link these levels clearly.

ENABLERS AND CONSTRAINTS

In one sense, many of the implications for HRM listed above are the factors that enable an effective link between HRM and performance. However, more detailed analysis shows that:

❖ relationships with colleagues/managers/support/ leadership are a key enabler at all stages of the process

❖ infrastructure – resources and staff – are important apart from at the final (performance) stage of the process

❖ professional ideology is important at all stages of the process and enables performance that might otherwise not be achieved

❖ access to a range of HR practices is also important at each stage of the process, including performance.

The various factors described throughout the Report as influences on the various elements of the framework are summarised in Table 21 on page 98, along with an indication of whether they are enablers of or constraints to the process, or whether their influence is context-dependent.

Although these findings may not be surprising, they do indicate that some enablers are not part of the traditional remit of the HR function or previously identified as HR practices. However, this presents many opportunities for the HR function to demonstrate its effectiveness as a 'business partner' in terms of supporting the organisation in achieving its goals.

Our findings suggest that there is no one 'best way' for HRM to operate in NHS organisations. Instead, HRM must become increasingly sophisticated in engaging with a range of stakeholders to enable improvements in performance.

Table 21 ❖ **How HRM influences performance – enablers and constraints**

		Enabler?	Constraint?	It depends...
HRM strategy: working with partners and contractors	Levels of institutional support which create a positive framework of governance and accountability	Yes		
	Senior managers at organisations across the network prepared to work positively with each other	Yes		
	Requirements that certain underlying principles of 'good' HRM govern the practices that contractors are expected to offer staff	Yes		
	Elements in commercial contracts that help to shape and sustain more positive effects	Yes		
	Close links between managers working for different employers	Yes		
	Poorer access for contracted staff to career development, appraisal and training opportunities		Yes	
	Lower levels of communication and involvement in change		Yes	
HRM content: the perceptions of individuals and the role of line managers	Single HR practices and combinations of practices			Yes
	Positive working relationships and close partnerships between line managers and the HR team	Yes		
	Good HR infrastructure	Yes		
	Line manager involvement in the development of HR policies	Yes		
	Lack of time		Yes	
	Unclear policies		Yes	
	Inadequate levels of expertise		Yes	
	Conflicting priorities		Yes	
The individual response to the HRM system	Support, clarity, leadership and supervision	Yes		
	Recognition	Yes		
	Physical environment, health and safety	Yes		
	Social environment: colleagues and team-work	Yes		
	Opportunity and support to deliver excellent patient care	Yes		
	Resources and time: having too much to do		Yes	
Performance	The professional ideology of staff	Yes		
	HR practices, specifically training and development	Yes		
	Help and encouragement from colleagues and managers	Yes		
	Feedback on performance	Yes		
	Infrastructure, specifically the level of staffing		Yes	
	Who employs the individual			Yes
	Individual emotions arising from having expectations met			Yes

APPENDIX 1 – METHODOLOGY

INTRODUCTION

Chapters 1 and 3 give details of the organisations involved in this research. We gathered data by interviewing a variety of staff, as well as analysing documents and observing some meetings. This appendix gives details of the questions asked in the various types of interviews we conducted and of how we gathered some background information. Details of who was interviewed are given in Chapter 1 ('Who we gathered the data from').

Prior to this empirical research we conducted two focus groups with participants on the Leadership Through Effective People Management development programme, funded by the NHS and provided by some of the research team members. This enabled us to clarify and agree the list of 11 HR practices which we then used within the case study organisations employee interviews (see Chapter 5).

We conducted three types of interview:

❖ access interviews – intended to gather contextual and background data specific to each case study organisation and held mainly with directors of the organisation concerned

❖ employee interviews – the majority of our sample – intended to gain individual perspectives on how HRM influences performance. These interviews comprised a series of questions and a card-sort to explore the way in which individuals thought that various HR practices related to each other and impacted on their own performance

❖ interviews with staff from partner and contractor organisations – intended to develop understanding of partnership and contracting arrangements in practice.

ACCESS INTERVIEWS

Access interviews were used to establish baseline data and provide an insight into the organisation. They were subsequently compared with documentary evidence such as the business and HR strategy documents, national performance data and any other documents gathered from the site. The interviews were structured to enable comparison across and within case sites.

Formal interview questions included:

1 What position do you hold in this Trust?

2 Organisational history – formation, organisation of services and departments, recent changes, local context?

3 Organisational strategy – main goals?

4 Use of contract staff and partnership arrangements?

5 How is performance measured – for the Trust and in your role? Are there any factors affecting organisational performance?

6 What is the HR strategy for the organisation?

7 Who is involved in developing HR strategy?

8 Structure of the HR department?

9 How is HRM delivered? Do HR policies cover all staff in the trust?

10 How does HRM affect performance?

EMPLOYEE INTERVIEWS

These interviews were aimed at gaining an idea of mental models of individuals' experiences within their work environment. The interview schedule adopted a loose structure guided by critical incidents and card-sorting techniques.

❖ The critical incident technique was developed by Flanagan (1954; p.327) as a 'set of procedures for collecting direct observations of human behaviour in such a way as to facilitate their potential usefulness in solving practical problems and developing broad psychological principles'.

❖ The visual card-sort technique (Daniels *et al*, 1995) is an adapted version because it requires the researcher to present the constructs to the individual to talk about rather than asking the individual to generate the constructs himself or herself. This enables individuals to use their own language to describe the constructs and how they might relate to their behaviour – it moves away from imposing a linear structure to participants' understandings (Mcdonald *et al*, 2004).

Formal questions included:

1 What position do you hold in this Trust?

Personal expectations

2 What do you expect your employer to provide?

❖ Have your expectations been met?

❖ How did this affect feelings, behaviour, performance, patient care?

Positive and negative incidents

3 Please give an example of both a positive and a negative incident you experienced at work during the last month

❖ How did this affect feelings, behaviour, performance, patient care?

Employer expectations

4 What does your employer expect of you?

❖ What helps or hinders you in meeting these expectations?

Going beyond expectations

5 Can you give an example of when you have gone beyond what is expected of you?

❖ What encouraged you to do this?

❖ Was there any impact on patient care?

Performance

6 What do you understand by the term 'performance'

❖ for the NHS?

❖ for the Trust/organisation?

❖ for your job?

Questions for managers:

7 In relation to the implementation of HR policies

❖ what is your involvement, precisely?

❖ what helps and what hinders implementation?

❖ is it part of appraisal?

HRM

8 What is HRM?

9 *The card-sort*, involving 11 cards each naming one aspect of HRM (appraisal; career development; communication between management and individuals; employee involvement in decision-making; job security; pay; recruitment; non-monetary rewards; teamworking; training; work–life balance) to be sorted according to

❖ how they enable you to do your job

❖ the way in which they relate together

CONTRACTOR/PARTNER INTERVIEWS

Questions for managers *not* employed by the NHS Trust but responsible for contracts that cut across organisational boundaries included:

1 Can you provide some background information about the nature of work undertaken/fields covered by the contract? Do these specifically state anything about NHS goals, in terms of effective patient care?

2 How is the contract managed?

3 Who is involved from each of the organisations involved?

4 What level are they in the relevant hierarchy?

5 Who decided on the terms of the contract and what to include?

6 How long is the contract for?

7 Is it a continuing contract or a one-off?

8 How is performance on the contract monitored?

9 Are there penalties for not hitting targets?

10 How can changes be made to the contract?

11 How well would you say the contract between your organisation and the NHS Trust actually works? Is the relationship based on trust and informality, arms'-length relations and formality, or what? [We would expect a mix of these, even in a single contract]

12 How many workers are included in the contract? How many work for your organisation and how many for the NHS Trust?

13 Do they work alongside each other doing the same or different jobs? Do they pass work to each other or do separate jobs?

With reference more specifically to HR issues:

1a How do HR policies and practices, and terms and conditions compare across the two (or more) organisations involved in this area of work. In particular, how well do they contribute to NHS goals of effective patient care?

Learning and development: quantity and quality of training and skills acquisition

1b Is there any joint training or similar qualifications for both sets of workers?

Pay and rewards: levels of pay and rewards, systems of payment

1c Is there a direct attempt to look at pay comparability?

Employee involvement (EI) and communications: forms of EI

1d Do workers employed by both organisations work in joint project teams, and how are these managed?

Recruitment and selection

1e How do the methods of recruitment and the quality of recruits compare?

Appraisal/career development: methods used

1f How do these compare across the two organisations?

Work–life balance

1g To what extent do both organisations emphasise issues to do with work–life balance?

Employment security

1h To what extent does each organisation guarantee employment security?

2 Are there tensions between the two (or more) organisations involved in this work/contract in terms of HR issues, or does it seem to work well, both from your perspective and that of your staff? Can you particularise any of the areas of HR from those covered above?

BACKGROUND DATA

Participants classified as employees (rather than access, partner or contractors) were required to complete a background questionnaire before they were interviewed. 146 out of 168 such employees completed the background questionnaire, resulting in a response rate of 87%. Table 22 shows response rates per case site.

The background questionnaire was used to collect the following information.

Sample demographics:

❖ gender

❖ tenure in job, in Trust and in the NHS

❖ pay band (if applicable).

Table 22 ❖ Response rates	
Case site	Rate
1 – Acute	78%
2 – Acute	89%
3 – Mental health	93%
4 – Mental health	90%
5 – Primary care	90%
6 – Primary care	83%
Total	87%

Table 23 ❖ Statements for rating responses	

Perceived organisational support (POS)	
The Trust fails to appreciate any extra effort from me	Low ratings indicate low levels of POS
The Trust supports me in providing what I need to do a good job	Low ratings indicate high levels of POS
Organisational citizenship behaviour (OCB)	
I am mindful of how my behaviour affects other people's work	Low ratings indicate high levels OCB
Organisational commitment (OC)	
I really feel as if the Trust's problems are my own	Low ratings indicate high levels of OC
Procedural justice (PJ)	
I think the way things are done is fair	Low ratings indicate high levels of PJ
Intention to leave	
I often think about leaving this Trust	Low ratings indicate intention to leave

Individuals were required to rate a series of statements on a scale of 1 to 5 (1 = strongly agree; 5 = strongly disagree). The statements, their descriptions and their interpretations are shown in Table 23 above.

ANOVA (job type, pay band, case, Trust type) and independent samples t-test (gender) were used to see if there were any significant differences between the mean score of participants from different job types, pay bands, case, Trust and based on gender. The results are shown at appropriate places throughout this report.

Participants were further required to place in order of importance to them (1 = most important; 5 = least important) the NHS, their Trust, their profession, their team and the patient.

RESEARCH WORKSHOPS

A series of three workshops were held in London, Birmingham and Manchester during March 2007. Preliminary findings of the research were presented to 45 senior NHS HR managers from a range of NHS organisations. The purpose of the workshops was:

❖ to present findings and seek reactions and observations on the findings

❖ to explore the implications for HR provision in the NHS

❖ to develop national policy implications

❖ to translate the findings into usable format through the Research Report.

Following each workshop the feedback was used both to modify the presentation of findings for future workshops and to incorporate feedback into the final report.

Workshops were chosen as an appropriate methodology because they are a powerful means to test new ideas and generate discussion with a wide range of people within a short time-frame. A key decision was to test the resonance of the findings with senior HR managers and directors across different sectors of the NHS. Workshops were organised through the CIPD.

Questions posed at workshops included:

❖ How can HR ensure that the individual and organisational benefits of HR practices are experienced?

❖ How can HR align changing individual and organisational expectations?

❖ How does HR strategy contribute to workforce development?

❖ What is the role of HR in contract/partnership relationships?

❖ How can HR become a valued activity for managers?

❖ How can flexible HR packages and processes be developed?

* How can HR work to link individual and organisational performance?

* What is the HR role in linking individual effort to patient care?

ETHICS

It is a requirement for all research involving NHS staff that ethics approval is granted through NHS research ethics committees. National multi-site ethical approval for this study was granted (ref: 05/Q2604/76). The research was also registered with the local Research and Development committee for each case study organisation.

There were two ethical issues of particular importance: informed consent and confidentiality. Each individual was provided with information about the study and the nature of the interview. They consented to being tape-recorded (with the exception of one participant – who gave an interview recorded in note form) and were able to withdraw participation at any time. Each transcript was assigned a code relating to case number, interview number and job title. Tapes and transcripts were all stored in locked filing cabinets and electronic files were stored on a secured area of the University of Manchester computer system.

DATA ANALYSIS

The approach used to analyse the data in this study followed a structured approach to demonstrate transparent analysis and allow for the extraction of valid proposals and findings from large data sets (Miles and Huberman, 1994). This was particularly important in assuring consistent data analysis between different researchers. Data analysis formed a continuous, iterative process throughout this phase of the study.

* Primary data was coded using the NVivo software package (QSR international), coded data being returned subsequently to Excel files because the size of the data set resulted in instability of the NVivo package. The research team collectively used codes based on the research questions and emerging themes.

* Emergent themes were discussed and developed at regular meetings of the research team, and for questions relating to individual perceptions the coding framework was extended and developed.

* These themes were then compared to existing themes in the literature

* Lead researchers for each case study organisation then summarised the data for their case site, and this data was contrasted across sites.

* Data was contrasted by Trust type, job type and pay band looking for differences and to allow broad conclusions to be drawn from the research findings.

* Data from the six sites were then integrated to provide in-depth comparative case material.

* Through this iterative process of data analysis, conclusions developed and became more explicit.

* Findings were verified through research workshops and through discussions of the coding framework between members of the research team.

APPENDIX 2 – INDIVIDUAL EXPECTATIONS

DATA ON INDIVIDUAL EXPECTATIONS

What does the data in the tables mean?

In the following tables (containing detailed data summarised in Chapters 7 and 8) we have weighted the figures by the case study organisation with the highest number of responses, so that each case is equally represented proportionately. This then enables comparisons between cases which would not otherwise be possible because of the different sample sizes at each case study organisation. All data shown has been weighted in this way.

In each table total percentages show each type of expectation as a proportion of all expectations.

Table 24 ❖ Explicit expectations across sites			
	HR practice	Help and encouragement	Infrastructure
Case 1: Acute	36 (18%)	24 (16%)	14 (15%)
Case 2: Acute	40 (20%)	22 (15%)	12 (12%)
Case 3: Mental Health	31 (16%)	28 (19%)	15 (15%)
Case 4: Mental Health	30 (15%)	29 (20%)	15 (15%)
Case 5: Primary Care Trust	26 (13%)	22 (15%)	27 (28%)
Case 6: Primary Care Trust	37 (19%)	22 (15%)	15 (15%)
Total	200 (45%)	147 (33%)	98 (22%)

Table 25 ❖ **Explicit HR practice expectations**

	Training	Appraisal	Pay	Career	Communications	Work–life balance	Security	Induction	Rewards	Staffing
Case 1: Acute	9 (12%)	0 (0%)	7 (44%)	7 (25%)	1 (8%)	0 (0%)	3 (50%)	0 (0%)	3 (30%)	3 (16%)
Case 2: Acute	16 (21%)	3 (50%)	3 (19%)	1 (4%)	3 (25%)	0 (0%)	0 (0%)	4 (31%)	1 (10%)	1 (5%)
Case 3: Mental Health	15 (19%)	2 (33%)	0 (0%)	7 (25%)	2 (17%)	1 (11%)	1 (17%)	2 (15%)	1 (10%)	0 (0%)
Case 4: Mental Health	13 (17%)	1 (17%)	2 (13%)	4 (14%)	2 (17%)	1 (11%)	2 (33%)	0 (0%)	1 (10%)	6 (32%)
Case 5: Primary Care Trust	15 (19%)	0 (0%)	3 (19%)	3 (11%)	2 (17%)	0 (0%)	0 (0%)	2 (15%)	2 (20%)	7 (37%)
Case 6: Primary Care Trust	10 (13%)	0 (0%)	1 (6%)	6 (21%)	2 (17%)	7 (78%)	0 (0%)	5 (38%)	2 (20%)	2 (11%)
Total	78 (40%)	6 (3%)	16 (8%)	28 (14%)	12 (6%)	9 (5%)	6 (3%)	13 (7%)	10 (5%)	19 (10%)

Table 26 ❖ **Explicit help and encouragement expectations**

	Support	Supervision	Clarity	Leadership
Case 1: Acute	9 (9%)	0 (0%)	16 (36%)	2 (20%)
Case 2: Acute	19 (20%)	2 (19%)	4 (9%)	2 (20%)
Case 3: Mental Health	14 (15%)	3 (27%)	8 (18%)	2 (20%)
Case 4: Mental Health	19 (20%)	2 (19%)	5 (11%)	1 (10%)
Case 5: Primary Care Trust	19 (20%)	0 (0%)	6 (14%)	2 (20%)
Case 6: Primary Care Trust	16 (17%)	4 (36%)	5 (11%)	1 (10%)
Total	96 (59%)	11 (7%)	44 (27%)	10 (6%)

Table 27 ❖ **Explicit infrastructure expectations**

	Physical environment	Social environment	Resources	Health and safety
Case 1: Acute	9 (16%)	0 (0%)	9 (16%)	2 (20%)
Case 2: Acute	9 (16%)	0 (0%)	9 (16%)	3 (30%)
Case 3: Mental Health	6 (11%)	0 (0%)	10 (18%)	5 (50%)
Case 4: Mental Health	11 (20%)	4 (80%)	6 (11%)	0 (0%)
Case 5: Primary Care Trust	8 (15%)	1 (20%)	12 (21%)	0 (0%)
Case 6: Primary Care Trust	11 (20%)	0 (0%)	10 (18%)	0 (0%)
Total	**54 (43%)**	**5 (4%)**	**56 (44%)**	**10 (8%)**

Table 28 ❖ **Individual expectations regarding employer expectations**

	Functional Commitment	Honesty	Reliability	Professional	Property	Flexibility	Loyalty	Don't know	Target/ Objectives	Leadership
Case 1: Acute	33 (23%)	0 (0%)	0 (0%)	3 (9%)	0 (0%)	0 (0%)	0 (0%)	0 (0%)	3 (43%)	0 (0%)
Case 2: Acute	22 (15%)	1 (11%)	0 (0%)	8 (24%)	0 (0%)	3 (33%)	1 (11%)	1 (33%)	1 (14%)	1 (8%)
Case 3: Mental Health	22 (15%)	1 (11%)	0 (0%)	9 (27%)	1 (100%)	3 (33%)	1 (11%)	0 (0%)	1 (14%)	1 (8%)
Case 4: Mental Health	17 (12%)	2 (22%)	1 (55%)	6 (18%)	0 (0%)	0 (0%)	4 (44%)	2 (66%)	0 (0%)	6 (50%)
Case 5: Primary Care Trust	32 (22%)	3 (33%)	0 (0%)	1 (3%)	0 (0%)	0 (0%)	0 (0%)	0 (0%)	1 (14%)	1 (8%)
Case 6: Primary Care Trust	20 (14%)	2 (22%)	1 (55%)	6 (18%)	0 (0%)	3 (33%)	3 (33%)	0 (0%)	1 (14%)	3 (25%)
Total	**146 (63%)**	**9 (4%)**	**2 (1%)**	**33 (14%)**	**1 (1%)**	**9 (4%)**	**9 (4%)**	**3 (1%)**	**7 (3%)**	**12 (5%)**

Table 29 ❖ Factors that help individuals to meet employer expectations

	HRM	Colleagues/team	Manager	Autonomy	Resources	Culture/image	Policies	Self	Encouragement	Other
Case 1: Acute	7 (24%)	10 (20%)	0 (0%)	4 (25%)	0 (0%)	0 (0%)	0 (0%)	7 (29%)	0 (0%)	0 (0%)
Case 2: Acute	1 (3%)	9 (19%)	4 (20%)	2 (13%)	1 (33%)	2 (22%)	2 (66%)	4 (17%)	0 (0%)	2 (29%)
Case 3: Mental Health	5 (17%)	5 (10%)	5 (25%)	0 (0%)	0 (0%)	4 (44%)	1 (33%)	4 (17%)	1 (33%)	1 (14%)
Case 4: Mental Health	5 (17%)	7 (15%)	2 (10%)	2 (13%)	2 (66%)	2 (22%)	0 (0%)	6 (25%)	0 (0%)	1 (14%)
Case 5: Primary Care Trust	5 (17%)	9 (19%)	4 (20%)	4 (25%)	0 (0%)	0 (0%)	0 (0%)	2 (8%)	3 (66%)	1 (14%)
Case 6: Primary Care Trust	6 (21%)	8 (17%)	5 (25%)	4 (25%)	0 (0%)	1 (11%)	0 (0%)	1 (4%)	0 (0%)	2 (29%)
Total	29 (18%)	48 (29%)	20 (12%)	16 (9%)	3 (2%)	9 (6%)	3 (2%)	24 (15%)	4 (2%)	7 (4%)

Table 30 ❖ What hinders employees from meeting employers' expectations

	Workload demands	Colleague/manager	HR practice	Targets	Environment	Lack of staff/resources	Administrative issues	Self	None	Other
Case 1: Acute	6 (16%)	0 (0%)	0 (0%)	2 (29%)	0 (0%)	4 (15%)	2 (22%)	0 (0%)	2 (8%)	10 (45%)
Case 2: Acute	5 (14%)	2 (29%)	5 (55%)	0 (0%)	2 (50%)	3 (12%)	2 (22%)	1 (17%)	3 (12%)	2 (9%)
Case 3: Mental Health	7 (19%)	2 (29%)	2 (22%)	0 (0%)	0 (0%)	7 (27%)	0 (0%)	0 (0%)	5 (20%)	2 (9%)
Case 4: Mental Health	6 (16%)	0 (0%)	1 (11%)	0 (0%)	0 (0%)	4 (15%)	3 (33%)	1 (17%)	10 (40%)	1 (5%)
Case 5: Primary Care Trust	9 (24%)	0 (0%)	1 (11%)	5 (71%)	1 (25%)	3 (12%)	1 (11%)	1 (17%)	1 (4%)	3 (14%)
Case 6: Primary Care Trust	4 (11%)	3 (43%)	0 (0%)	0 (0%)	1 (25%)	5 (19%)	1 (11%)	3 (50%)	4 (16%)	4 (18%)
Total	37 (24%)	7 (5%)	9 (6%)	7 (5%)	4 (3%)	26 (17%)	9 (6%)	6 (4%)	25 (16%)	22 (14%)

Table 31 ❖ **Examples of going beyond what was expected**

	Hours	Work	Persist	Volunteer	Help	Nothing is beyond	Other
Case 1: Acute	11 (26%)	0 (0%)	0 (0%)	5 (18%)	2 (13%)	1 (7%)	9 (19%)
Case 2: Acute	2 (5%)	0 (0%)	4 (44%)	4 (15%)	4 (25%)	7 (47%)	8 (17%)
Case 3: Mental Health	6 (14%)	3 (25%)	3 (33%)	5 (18%)	0 (0%)	2 (13%)	9 (19%)
Case 4: Mental Health	8 (19%)	1 (8%)	1 (11%)	5 (18%)	5 (31%)	4 (27%)	3 (6%)
Case 5: Primary Care Trust	7 (16%)	3 (25%)	0 (0%)	7 (26%)	3 (19%)	1 (7%)	8 (17%)
Case 6: Primary Care Trust	9 (21%)	5 (42%)	1 (11%)	1 (4%)	2 (13%)	0 (0%)	10 (21%)
Total	**43 (25%)**	**12 (7%)**	**9 (5%)**	**27 (16%)**	**16 (9%)**	**15 (9%)**	**47 (28%)**

REFERENCES

ANDERSON, N. AND SCHALK, R. (1998)

'The psychological contract in retrospect and prospect'. *Journal of Organizational Behavior*, Vol.19, Special issue: The psychological contract at work: 637–47.

ARAH, O. A., KLATZINGER, N. S., DELNOIJ, D. M., ASHBROEK, A. H. A. T. and CUSTERS, T. (2003)

'Conceptual frameworks for health systems performance: a quest for effectiveness, quality and improvement'. *International Journal of Quality in Health Care*, Vol. 15, No. 5: 377–98.

BACKOFF, R. W. and NUTT, P. C. (1992)

Strategic Management of Public and Third Sector Organisations: A handbook for leaders. San Francisco: Jossey-Bass.

BALLANTINE, J., BRIGNALL, S. and MODELL, S. (1998)

'Performance measurement and management in public health services: a comparison of UK and Swedish practice'. *Management Accounting Research*, Vol. 9, No. 1: 710–94.

BOADEN, R., MARCHINGTON, M., HYDE, P., HARRIS, C., SPARROW, P., PASS, S., CARROLL, M. and CORTVRIEND, P. (2007)

Improving Health through Human Resource Management: Summary. London: Chartered Institute of Personnel and Development.

BORMAN, W. C. and MOTOWIDLO, S. J. (1993)

'Expanding the criterion domain to include elements of contextual performance'. In N. SCHMITT and W. C. BORMAN (eds) *Personnel Selection in Organisations.* San Francisco, CA: Jossey-Bass.

BOSELIE, P., DIETZ, G. and BOON, C. (2005)

'Commonalities and contradictions in HRM and performance research'. *Human Resource Management Journal*, Vol. 15, No. 3: 67–94.

BOWEN, D. E. and OSTROFF, C. (2004)

'Understanding HRM–firm performance linkages: the role of the "strength" of the HRM system'. *Academy of Management Review*, Vol. 29, No. 2: 203–21.

BOXALL, P. and PURCELL, J. (2003)

Strategy and Human Resource Management. Houndmills, Palgrave Macmillan.

BOYNE, G. A. (1996)

'The intellectual crisis in British public administration: is public management the problem or the solution?' *Public Administration*, Vol. 74. No 4: 679–94.

BOYNE, G. A. (2002a)

'Public and private management: what's the difference?' *Journal of Management Studies*, Vol. 39, No. 1, January: 97–122.

BOYNE, G. A. (2002b)

'Concepts and indicators of local authority performance: an evaluation of the statutory frameworks in England and Wales'. *Public Money and Management*, Vol. 22, No. 2, Apr-Jun: 17–24.

BOYNE, G. A. (2003)

'Sources of public service improvement: a critical review and research agenda'. *Journal of Public Administration Research and Theory*, Vol. 13, No. 3, Juy: 367–94.

BRUNSWIK, E. (1956)

Perception and the Representative Design of Psychological Experiments. Berkeley, CA: University of California Press.

BUCHANAN, D. A, FITZGERALD, L. and KETLEY, D. (EDS) (2007)

The Sustainability and Spread of Organizational Change. Abingdon: Routledge.

BUNDERSON, J. S. (2001)

'How work ideologies shape the psychological contracts of professional employees: Doctors' responses to perceived breach'. *Journal of Organizational Behavior*, Vol. 22, No. 7: 717–41.

CAMPBELL, S. M., ROLAND, M. O. and BUETOW, S. A. (2000)

'Defining quality of care'. *Social Science and Medicine*, Vol. 51, No. 11: 1611–25.

COMBS, J., LIU, Y., HALL, A. and KETCHEN, D. (2006)

'How much do high performance work practices matter? A meta-analysis of their effects on organizational performance'. *Personnel Psychology*, Vol. 59, No 3: 501–28.

CONFEDERATION OF BRITISH INDUSTRY (2006)

Working Together: Embedding good employment in public services. London: CBI.

CONWAY, N. (1996)

'The psychological contract: a metaphor too far?' British Academy of Management Conference, Bradford.

COX, A., MARCHINGTON, M. and SUTER, J. (2007)

Embedding the Provision of Information and Consultation in the Workplace: A longitudinal analysis of employee outcomes in 1998 and 2004. DTI Employment Relations Research Series, No 72.

CULLINANE, N., and DUNDON, T. (2006)

'The psychological contract: a critical review'. *International Journal of Management Reviews*, Vol. 8. No 2: 113–29.

DANIELS, K., DE CHERNATONY, C. and JOHNSON, G. (1995)

'Validating a method for mapping managers' mental models of competition'. *Human Relations*, Vol. 48, No 9: 975–91

DEPARTMENT OF HEALTH (2000)

The NHS Plan: A plan for investment, a plan for reform. London: Department of Health.

DEPARTMENT OF HEALTH (2005)

A National Framework to Support Local Workforce Strategy Development: A guide for DH directors in the NHS. London: Department of Health.

DEPARTMENT OF HEALTH (2006a)

HR High Impact Changes: An evidence-based resource. London: Department of Health.

DEPARTMENT OF HEALTH (2006b)

Commissioning a Patient-led NHS. London: Department of Health.

DEPARTMENT OF HEALTH (2007)

The NHS in England: The operating framework for 2007/8. London: Department of Health.

DOMBERGER, S., JENSEN, P. H. and STONECASH, R. E. (2002)

'Examining the magnitude and sources of cost savings associated with outsourcing'. *Public Performance and Management Review*, Vol. 26, No. 2: 148–68.

DONABEDIAN, A. (1980)

The Definition of Quality and Approaches to Its Assessment. Chicago, IL: Health Administration Press.

EARNSHAW, J., MARCHINGTON, M. and GOODMAN J. (2000)

'Unfair to whom? Discipline and dismissal in small establishments'. *Industrial Relations Journal*, Vol. 31, No. 1: 62–73.

EISENBERGER, R., STINGLHAMBER, F., VANDENGERHE, C., SUCHARSK, I. and ROADES, L. (2002)

'Perceived supervisor support: contributions to perceived organisational support and employee retention'. *Journal of Applied Psychology*, Vol. 87, No. 3: 565–73.

EISENHARDT, T. K. (1989)

'Building theory from case study research'. *Academy of Management Review*, Vol. 14, No. 4: 32–50.

FERLIE, E. and MCGIVERN, G. (2003)

Relationships Between Health Care Organisations: A critical review of the literature and a research agenda. London: National Co-ordinating Centre for NHS Service Delivery and Organisation.

FIOL, C. M., O'CONNOR, E. J. and AGUINIS H. (2001)

'All for one and one for all? The development and transfer of power across organizational levels'. *Academy of Management Review*, Vol. 26, No. 2: 224–42.

FITZGERALD, L., LILLEY, C., FERLIE, E., ADDICOTT, R., MCGIVERN, G. and BUCHANAN, D. (2006)

Managing Change and Role Enactment in the Professionalised Organisation. London: National Co-ordinating Centre for NHS Service Delivery and Organisation, Research and Development.

FLANAGAN, J. C. (1954)

'The critical incident technique'. *Psychological Bulletin*, Vol. 51, No. 4: 327–59.

FLOOD, A. B. (1994)

'The impact of organisational and managerial factors on the quality of care in health care organisations'. *Medical Care Review*, Vol. 51, No. 4: 381–429.

FOLKARD, S. and LOMBARDI, D. A. (2006)

'Modelling the impact of the components of long hours on injuries and "accidents"'. *American Journal of Industrial Medicine*, Vol. 49, No. 11: 953–63.

FULOP, N., SCHEIBL, F. and EDWARDS, N. (2004)

Turnaround in Health Care Providers. London: London School of Hygiene and Tropical Medicine.

GLYNN., J. J. and MURPHY, M. P. (1996)

'Public management: failing accountabilities and failing performance review'. *International Journal of Public Sector Management*, Vol. 9, No 5/6: 125–37.

GUEST, D. E. and CONWAY, N. (2004)

Employee Well-Being and the Psychological Contract. London: CIPD.

HARRIS, C., CORTVRIEND, P. and HYDE, P. (2007)

'Human resource management and performance in healthcare organisations'. *Journal of Healthcare Organisation and Management* (in press).

HARTLEY, J. (2004)

'Case study research'. In CASSELL, C. and SYMON, G. (eds) *Essential Guide to Qualitative Methods in Organizational Research.* London: Sage.

HARVEY, G., HYDE, P. and WALSHE, K. (2004)

Investigating Turnaround in the NHS Organisational Supported by the Performance Development Team of the Modernisation Agency. Manchester: Manchester Business School.

HENDRY, C., PETTIGREW, A. and SPARROW, P. R. (1989)

'Linking strategic change, competitive performance and human resource management: results of a UK empirical study'. In R. MANSFIELD (ed.) *Frontiers of Management Research*. London: Routledge.

HERRIOT, P., MANNING, W.E.G. and KIDD, M. (1997)

'The content of the psychological contract' *British Journal of Management* 8, 151–62

HODGKINSON, G. and SPARROW, P. R. (2002)

The Competent Organization: A psychological analysis of the strategic management process. Milton Keynes: Open University Press.

HOOD, C. (1991)

'A new public management for all seasons?'. *Public Administration*, Vol. 69, No. 1: 3–19.

HUTCHINSON, S. and PURCELL, J. (2003)

Bringing Policies to Life: The vital role of front line managers. London: Chartered Institute of Personnel and Development.

HYDE, P., BOADEN, R., CORTVRIEND, P., HARRIS, C., MARCHINGTON, M., PASS, S., SPARROW, P. and SIBBALD, B. (2006a)

Improving Health through Human Resource Management: Mapping the territory. London: Chartered Institute of Personnel and Development and the Department of Health.

HYDE, P., BOADEN, R., CORTVRIEND, P., HARRIS, C., MARCHINGTON, M., PASS, S., SPARROW, P. and SIBBALD, B. (2006b)

Improving Health through Human Resource Management: A starting point for change. London: Chartered Institute of Personnel and Development.

JOHNSON, R. and CLARK, G. (2005)

Service Operations Management, 2nd edition. Harlow: Prentice Hall.

KAPLAN, R. S. and NORTON, D. P. (1996)

The Balanced Scorecard – Translating strategy into action. Boston, MA: Harvard Business School Press.

KLEIN, M. W., MALONE, M. F., BENNIS, W. G. and BERKOWITZ, N. H. (1961)

'Problems of measuring patient care in the out-patient department'. *Journal of Health and Human Behavior*, Vol. 2, No. 2, Summer: 138–44.

LAM, W., HUANG, X. and SNAPE, E. (2007)

'Feedback-seeking behaviour and leader-member exchange: do supervisor attributed motives matter?' *Academy of Management Journal*, Vol. 50, No. 2: 348–63.

LASCHINGER, J., FINEGAN, J. and SHAMIAN, J. (2001)

'The impact of workplace empowerment, organizational trust on staff nurses' work satisfaction and organizational commitment'. *Health Care Management Review*, Vol. 26, No. 3: 7–23.

LEONARD, M., GRAHAM, S. and BONACUM, D. (2004)

'The human factor: the critical importance of effective teamwork and communication in providing safe care'. *Quality and Safety in Health Care*, Vol. 13, No. 5: 85–90.

LESTER, S. W., TURNLEY, W. H., BLOODGOOD, J. M. and BOLINO, M. C. (2002)

'Not seeing eye to eye: differences in supervisor and subordinate perceptions of an attribution for psychological contract breech'. *Journal of Organizational Behavior*, Vol. 23, No. 1: 39–56.

LIDEN, R. C., SPARROWE, R. T. and WAYNE, S. J. (1997)

'Leader–member exchange theory: the past and potential for the future'. In G. R. FERNS (ed.) *Research in Personnel and Human Resource Management*, Vol. 15. Stamford, CT: JAI Press.

LILFORD, R., MOHAMMED, A. M., SPIEGELHALTER, D. and THOMSON, R. (2004)

'Use and misuse of process and outcome data in managing performance of acute medical care: avoiding institutional stigma'. *The Lancet*, Vol. 363, No. 9415, April: 1147–54.

MANNION, R., DAVIES, H. and MARSHALL, M. (2005)

'Impact of star performance ratings in English acute hospital Trusts'. *Journal of Health Services Research and Policy*, Vol. 10, No. 1: 18–24.

MARCHINGTON, M. and GRUGULIS, I. (2000)

'Best practice human resource management: perfect opportunity or dangerous illusion?' *International Journal of Human Resource Management*, Vol. 11, No. 6: 1104–24.

MARCHINGTON, M., GRIMSHAW, D., RUBERY, J. and WILLMOTT, H. (EDS) (2005)

Fragmenting Work: Blurring organisational boundaries and disordering hierarchies. Oxford: Oxford University Press.

MARCHINGTON, M. and WILKINSON, A. (2005)

'Direct participation'. In S. BACH and K. SISSON (eds) *Personnel Management: A comprehensive guide to theory and practice*. Oxford: Blackwell.

MAYLOR, H. and BLACKMON, K. (2005)

Researching Business and Management. Basingstoke: Palgrave Macmillan.

MCDONALD, S., DANIELS, K. and HARRIS, C. (2004)

'Mapping methods for organizational research'. In CASSELL, C. and SYMON, G. (eds) *Essential Guide to Qualitative Methods in Organisational Research*. London: Sage.

MCGOVERN, P., GRATTON, L., HOPE-HAILEY, V., STILES, P. and TRUSS, C. (1997)

'Human resource management on the line?' *Human Resource Management Journal*, Vol. 7, No. 4, July: 12–29.

MEYER, J. P., ALLEN, N. J. and SMITH, C. A. (1993)

'Commitment to organizations and occupations: extension and test of a three component conceptualization'. *Journal of Applied Psychology*, Vol. 78, No, 4: 538–51.

MILES, M. and HUBERMAN, A. (1994)

Qualitative Data Analysis. Newbury Park, CA: Sage.

MINTZBERG, H. (1979)

The Structuring of Organizations: A synthesis of the research. Englewood Cliffs, NJ: Prentice Hall.

MINTZBERG, H. (2003)

'The professional organization'. In MINTZBERG, H., LAMPEL, J., QUINN, J. B. and GHOSHAL, J. B. (eds) *Strategy Process: Concepts, contexts, cases.* Harlow: Pearson Education.

MORGAN, P., ALLINGTON, N. and HEERY, E. (2000)

'Employment insecurity in the public services'. In E. HEERY and J. SALMON (eds) *The Insecure Workforce.* London: Routledge.

NHS CONFEDERATION (2007a)

Great Expectations: What does customer focus mean for the NHS? London: NHS Confederation.

NHS CONFEDERATION (2007b)

The Challenges of Leadership in the NHS. London: NHS Confederation.

NORMAN, D. A. (1983)

'Some observations on mental models'. In GENTNER, D. and STEVENS, A. L. (eds) *Mental Models.* Hillsdale, NJ: Erlbaum.

NORREKLIT, H. (2000)

'The balance on the balanced scorecard – a critical analysis of some of its assumptions'. *Management Accounting Research*, Vol. 11, No 1: 65–88.

OTHMAN, R., ARSHAD, R., HASHIM, N. A. and ROSMAH, M. (2005)

'Psychological contract violation and organizational citizenship behavior'. *Gadjah Mada International Journal of Business*, Vol. 7. No. 3: 325–49.

PETTIGREW, A. M. and WHIPP, R. (1991)

Managing Change for Competitive Success. Oxford: Blackwell.

PETTIGREW, A. M., FERLIE, E. and MCKEE, L. (1992)

Shaping Strategic Change – Making change in large organisations: The case of the NHS. London: Sage.

PIERSON, P. (2003)

'Big, slow-moving, and ... invisible'. In MAHONEY, J. and RUESCHEMEYER, D. (eds) *Comparative Historical Analysis in the Social Sciences.* Cambridge: Cambridge University Press.

PODSAKOFF, P. M., and MACKENZIE, S. B. (1997)

'Impact of organizational citizenship behavior on organizational performance: a review and suggestions for future research'. *Human Performance*, Vol. 10. No. 2: 133–51.

POWELL, M., BROCK, D. and HININGS, C. (1999)

'The changing professional organisation'. In D. BROCK, M. POWELL and C. HININGS (eds) *Restructuring the Professional Organisation: Accounting, care and law.* London: Routledge.

PURCELL, J., KINNIE, N., HUTCHINSON, S., RAYTON, B. and SWART J. (2003)

Understanding the People and Performance Link: Unlocking the black box. London: Chartered Institute of Personnel and Development.

RAMANUJAM, R. and ROUSSEAU, D. (2006)

'The challenges are organizational, not just clinical'. *Journal of Organizational Behavior*, Vol. 27, No. 7: 811–27.

ROBINSON, S. L. and MORRISON, E. W. (2000)

'The development of psychological contract breach and violation: a longitudinal study'. *Journal of Organizational Behavior*, Vol. 21, No. 5: 525–46.

ROGERS, A. E., HWANG. W., SCOTT, L. D., AIKEN, L. and DINGES, D. F. (2004)

'The working hours of hospital staff nurses and patient safety'. *Health Affairs*, Vol. 23, No. 4, July/Aug: 202–12.

ROUSE, W. B. and MORRIS, N. M. (1986)

'On looking into the black box: prospects and limits in the search for mental models'. *Psychological Bulletin*, Vol. 100, No. 3: 349–63.

ROUSSEAU, D. M. (1995)

Psychological Contracts in Organizations: Understanding written and unwritten agreements. Thousand Oaks, CA: Sage.

ROUSSEAU, D. (2001)

'Schema, promise and mutuality: the building blocks of the psychological contract'. *Journal of Occupational and Organisational Psychology*, Vol. 74, No. 4: 511–41.

SCHEIN, E. H. (1978)

Career Dynamics: Matching individual and organisational needs. Reading, MA: Addison-Wesley.

SCOTT, T., MANNION, R., MARSHALL, M. and DAVIES, H. (2003)

'Does organisational culture influence healthcare performance? A review of the evidence'. *Journal of Health Services Research and Policy*, Vol. 8, No. 2, April: 105–17.

SPARKS, K., COOPER, C., FRIED, Y. and SHIROM, A. (1997)

'The effects of hours at work on health: a meta-analytic review'. *Journal of Occupational and Organizational Psychology*, Vol. 70, No. 4: 391–408.

SPARROW, P. and COOPER, C. L. (2003)

The Employment Relationship: Key challenges for HR. London: Butterworth-Heinemann.

THE HEALTH COMMITTEE (2007)

Workforce Planning: Fourth report of session 2006/7. London: House of Commons, The Stationery Office.

THOMPSON, J. A. and BUNDERSON, J. T. (2003)

'Violations of principle: Ideological currency in the psychological contract'. *Academy of Management Review*, Vol. 28, No. 4: 571–86.

TRUSS C. (2001)

'Complexities and controversies in linking HRM with organisational outcomes'. *Journal of Management Studies*, Vol. 38, No. 8: 1121–49.

TURNLEY, W. H. and FELDMAN, D. C. (1999)

'A discrepancy model of psychological contract violations'. *Human Resource Management Review*, Vol. 9. No. 3: 367–86.

ULRICH, D. (1997)

Human Resource Champions: The next agenda for adding value and delivering results. Boston, MA: Harvard University Press.

VAN DE VEN, A. H. and POOLE, M. S. (2002)

'Field research methods'. In J. A. C. BAUM (ed.) *Companion to Organizations*. Oxford: Blackwell.

VERE, D. (2005)

Fit for Business: Building a strategic HR function in the public sector. London: CIPD.

WATSON, D., CLARK, L. A. and TELLEGEN, A. (1988)

'Development and validation of brief measures of positive and negative affect: the PANAS scales'. *Journal of Personality and Social Psychology*, Vol. 54, No. 6: 1063–70.

WEST, M. A., BORRILL, C., DAWSON, J., SCULLY, J., CARTER, M., ANELAY, S., PATTERSON, M. and WARING, J. (2002)

'The link between the management of employees and patient mortality in acute hospitals'. *International Journal of Human Resource Management*, Vol. 13, No. 8: 1299–1310.

WEST, M. A., GUTHRIE, J. P., DAWSON, J., BORRILL, C. S. and CARTER, M. (2006)

'Reducing patient mortality in hospitals: the role of human resource management'. *Journal of Organizational Behavior*, Vol. 27, No. 7: 983–1022.

WHITTAKER, S. and MARCHINGTON, M. (2003)

'Devolving HR responsibility to the line: threat, opportunity or partnership?', *Employee Relations*, Vol. 36, No 3: 245–61.

WRIGHT, P. M. and HAGGERTY, J. J. (2005)

'Missing variables in theories of strategic human resource management: time, cause and individuals'. Working Paper 05-03. Ithaca, NY: Cornell University.

YIN, R. K. (1994)

Applications of Case Study Research. London: Sage.